# THEY
# NEVER
# SURRENDERED

ALLIED POWS WHO DEFIED THEIR CAPTORS
IN WORLD WAR II IN HONG KONG & JAPAN
1941-1945

D1601270

Design: Sue Beard
Printer: ORBIT Design Services

MacDonell, George S.
    **They Never Surrendered** *Allied POWs who defied their Captors in World War II in Hong Kong & Japan 1941-1945/* George S. MacDonell.

Printed and bound in Canada
www.orbitdesignservices.com
V#23.

ORBIT Design Services
946 Lawrence Ave. E. PO Box 47622
Toronto, ON M3C 3S7
416-444-2818

**Other Books by George MacDonell:**
    **A Dog Named GANDER**
    George S. MacDonell & Sue Beard
    www.ADogNamedGANDER.com

    **George...The Life and Times of George S MacDonell**
    George S. MacDonell
    www.volumesdirect.com/detail.aspx?ID=5350

    **One Soldier's Story**
    George S. MacDonell

# THEY NEVER SURRENDERED

ALLIED POWS WHO DEFIED THEIR CAPTORS
IN WORLD WAR II IN HONG KONG & JAPAN
1941-1945

*Take these men for your example.*
*Like them, remember that*
*Prosperity can be only for the free,*
*That Freedom is the sure possession*
*of those alone who have the*
*Courage to defend it.*

PERICLE'S FUNERAL ORATION TO THE ATHENIANS
431 B.C.

# Table of Contents

# *Foreword*

It is an honour for me to write this foreword for George MacDonell's latest book They Never Surrendered - Allied POWs who defied their Captors in WWII in Hong Kong & Japan 1941-1945. This book is about the soldiers of "C-Force", of which George was one, who fought so bravely against impossible odds to defend the island of Hong Kong in 1941. George MacDonell continues to inform Canadians of the story of "C Force" in Hong Kong and the soldiers who fought so bravely and courageously and of those who endured impossible conditions as prisoners of war for four years.

These individual profiles portray the courage and the spirit of those who, while defeated on the battlefield and forced to become prisoners of war, never gave up their patriotism or their determination to defy their brutal enemy.

It is an added honour for me because my father, Brigadier J.K. Lawson, was the Commanding Officer of "C-Force" and it was there in Hong Kong, with his men, that he was killed in action. When his headquarters was surrounded by the Japanese, on 19 December, rather than surrender, he left his bunker "to fight it out." Those were his last words.

I have always been very proud of all the Canadians of "C-Force" who fought with such courage and determination and who carried on the fight even from their prison camps, until almost four years later, when the allied victory set them free.

I know my father would be proud of their place in our history, and to know that the soldiers of his command, by their courage and brave conduct, showed the world, in that bloody conflict, the mettle of which they were made.

John Lawson LCol
The Royal Canadian Regiment

# Preface

I was honoured when George MacDonell requested me to assist him with his latest book to record more of his recollections of the defence of Hong Kong, and those terrible days as a prisoner of war from 1941 to 1945. His memories of the events candidly tell the reader what these Canadians, who were a "band of brothers," did and endured, while in action on one of the world's most difficult battlefields. While he and his comrades were ordered to surrender: he makes it clear that they did *not* surrender! they continued fighting their savage enemy using their wits, ingenuity and any methods they could utilize to resist, sabotage and disrupt their war efforts. All this resistance was done under the most dangerous circumstances and always with the greatest risk of beatings, unspeakable torture and slow painful deaths–if caught. Examples of this treatment are accurately described and illustrated.

A book recording the brave actions of several of the many prisoners of war who did what they could against all odds to carry on fighting the Japanese after being captured, has been long overdue. I commend George for his initiative to tell in his own words several of those important stories. This book is a deserving tribute to the memory of those brave men.

Since 1978, I have been involved with telling various aspects of the many-faceted story of Canada's "C-Force" with my exhibits, illustrated presentations and writings. Over the years I have had the privilege to meet several hundred members of the Force, and become good friends with many of them. After they came to know me, they were willing to share their war time experiences, the struggles they went through to regain their health, their postwar successes and lives in general. I consider them to be some of the bravest, most talented and skilled men I have ever known and believe they are all; "great" Canadians and, true "heroes."

C.R. McGuire

11

# *Acknowlegements*

First, I would like to thank Jon Reid, Colonel John Lawson and Judy Bunch for their special help in writing this book. They gave me background stories and insights into three great leaders who fought for our freedom – their fathers – Major John Reid, Brigadier John Lawson and Lieutenant Commander Jerry Bunch, USN. Their memories, which began in childhood, were very helpful in learning so much more about these three largely unknown heroes.

Special thanks goes to Ron McGuire, who from the very beginning, contributed so much by his careful research and data gathering. He was invaluable in every aspect of this work for his encouragement and his unstinting support and wise counsel.

I also wish to thank my good friends Graham Young and John Rosolak. Graham, for sharing his expertise as an accomplished author, and John, the noted military historian, for sharing his extensive knowledge of our military history.

And finally, I would like to thank Sue Beard for her invaluable help in every aspect of this work.

George MacDonell

*Sergeant G.S.MacDonell, Royal Rifles of Canada, Valcartier Québéc, 1941*

# Introduction

On the 23 December 1941, two days before hostilities ended, Prime Minister Churchill sent an order to the defenders of Hong Kong. His order, in part, stated:

> *"There must be no thought of surrender....*
> *every day that you are able to maintain your resistance,*
> *you help the allied cause all over the world."* *

This is the story of the Canadian survivors of the Battle of Hong Kong who, after being defeated on the battlefield, became prisoners of war of the Japanese on Christmas day 1941. It is a portrayal of the Canadian spirit which refused to submit to the demands and cruelty of brutal captors. It tells of the courage and determination of these unbowed Canadian soldiers who, despite starvation and forced labour, obeyed their orders and defied and obstructed their enemy in every way they could. They may have lost the battle of Hong Kong against overwhelming odds, but their patriotism and their sense of duty to their country to carry on the fight remained undiminished. As POWs thrown into horrendous circumstances, they persisted in their refusal to give up or submit to their enemy for nearly four years, until the surrender of Japan in August 1945 set them free. Most of all, theirs is a story about the resilience, strength and courage of the human spirit - about never giving up and never admitting defeat. These men were my comrades. I served with them. I knew them well.

George MacDonell

* *Appendix A*

CHAPTER 1

# "C-Force" to Hong Kong

In September 1941, two years after World War II began, the Canadian Government received a request from Great Britain to send Canadian soldiers to reinforce the British garrison of Hong Kong.

The government of Canada complied with this request and in October of that year two Canadian Regiments were sent to Hong Kong: the Royal Rifles of Canada and the Winnipeg Grenadiers, accompanied by a Brigade Headquarters. Commanded by Brigadier J.K. Lawson, "C-Force," as the contingent was designated, was comprised of 1,975 officers and men and two nurses. After a long sea voyage the Canadians arrived in Hong Kong to take up their duties on November 16, 1941.

Hong Kong is a mountainous, irregularly-shaped island approximately 11 miles long and three miles wide lying just off the coast of South China, 90 miles south of Canton (Guangzhou). The island had been an important Crown Colony and colonial outpost of Great Britain since 1841. When "C-Force" arrived a century later, its 29 square miles were inhabited by a Chinese population of 1,100,000 citizens living under British protection.

By 1941, Hong Kong's military garrison was seriously under strength for an island of its size and importance. Including the newly arrived Canadians, its total military force consisted of 6,000 British, Indian and Canadian soldiers and 4,000 local police and militia defenders. There were also small contingents of the Royal Air Force and the Royal Navy, equipped with a few outmoded airplanes and small naval vessels.

Aside from weakness in numbers, the defense plans and narrow assumptions of the British authorities in command at Hong Kong were not reassuring to the newly arrived Canadians, who also found themselves treated with a certain British superciliousness reserved for "colonials." The British plan called for a thin, all-around perimeter defense of the island instead of strategic defenses concentrated on the high ground which would maximize the effectiveness of such a limited defense force. The Canadian officers of "C-Force", most of whom were decorated and highly experienced combat veterans of World War I, found the British plan wrong-headed and alarming. When these concerns were expressed to General Maltby, the British Garrison Commander, he told the Canadians not to worry. The Japanese were no real threat, he said, because of their generally poor eyesight. As it turned out, the real blindness in this situation was the complacent, contemptuous attitude that Maltby exemplified.

Overwhelmingly superior in strength and preparedness, the Japanese forces, which had been massing at Canton for several months before hostilities began, consisted of 60,000 soldiers of the 13th Japanese Field Army, supported by a large air force, naval and combat engineering components. As well as outnumbering the Hong Kong defenders by approximately six to one, the Japanese, having invaded Manchuria in 1931 and overrun large parts of China since

1937, were a battle-hardened and formidable foe. Canada, with no military intelligence of its own, was dependent on British military evaluations and assessments of the Far East military situation. And herein lies the seed of tragedy for the two gallant Canadian regiments posted to Hong Kong, almost as a military afterthought: due to its ultimate indefensibility to Japanese attack by the fall of 1941, the Canadian troops should never been sent to Hong Kong in the first place.

This fateful preamble to the story begins nine months earlier, in January 1941, when British Prime minister Winston Churchill was asked by General Hastings Ismay, Chief of the British Defense Staff, for permission to reinforce the garrison at Hong Kong.

A sage and prescient Churchill replied:

*Winston Churchill, c 1941.*

*This is all wrong. If Japan goes to war with us, there is not the slightest chance of holding Hong Kong or relieving it. It is most unwise to increase the loss we shall suffer there. Instead of increasing the garrison, it ought to be reduced to a symbolic scale. Any trouble arising there must be dealt with at the peace conference after the war. We must avoid frittering away our resources on unattainable positions. Japan will think long before declaring war on the British empire and whether there are two or six battalions at Hong Kong will make no difference to her choice. I wish we had fewer troops there, but to move any would be noticeable and dangerous.*

Besides the huge discrepancy in the number of combatants available to each side, Churchill's chillingly accurate assessment was based on a number of unalterable weaknesses in Hong Kong's position. Out of necessity, the island imported almost 95 per cent of its fresh water and food from mainland China. Hong Kong's military airport was also located on the mainland, and highly vulnerable to a land-based or air attack. As well, Hong Kong's major defenses were founded on the assumption that a Japanese attack would come from the sea: all of Hong Kong's heavy naval guns pointed seaward. As Japanese planners already knew and would soon exploit, in an invasion from the Chinese mainland the big guns could not be swung landward nor their barrels sufficiently elevated to bring fire to bear on Hong Kong's mountainous heights, from where land attacks would be launched once the Japanese were on

*Prime Minister Mackenzie King.*

the island. Finally, much of the island's original air and naval forces had been transferred south to Singapore, leaving the island's forces almost bereft of these supporting arms.

Ignored by the Canadian government when making its decision to send troops, Churchill's grim facts were soon discerned by the newly-arrived Canadians. Within two weeks of landing at Hong Kong, the Canadian Command had concluded that in the event of war with Japan and a

Japanese invasion of the Crown Colony the Royal Rifles and Grenadiers would be trapped: they could not be reinforced, they could not be re-supplied, they could not be evacuated. The Canadians would have two options: to die on the battlefield, or surrender to an enemy that had refused to sign the Geneva Convention on the treatment of prisoners of war, and whose recent history of savage behaviour in China erased any hope for humane treatment of Japanese prisoners in this conflict.

*General Arthur Grassett.*

Given all that was known at the time, why was Churchill's warning ignored? Why did the Government of Canada agree to send two thousand soldiers to their probable doom? The reasons leading to this quite avoidable military disaster are to be found in the murky tensions of Canadian politics and the jingoistic attitude of two ambitious generals. For some time Canadian Prime Minister Mackenzie King had been the object of hawkish criticism because, by now, two years since the start of the war, Canadian troops had still not been deployed in battle. Commonwealth troops from Australia, New Zealand, South Africa and India had been engaged by this time against the axis powers, but not Canadians. Some of King's own Liberal Cabinet members, including J.L. Ralston, Minister of National Defense, bombarded him with demands to blood Canadian troops. While King, highly sensitive to the reluctance of Francophones to become engaged in foreign wars, was delaying a commitment of Canadian troops to battle until absolutely necessary, ill-founded discussions were going on behind his back in Ottawa.

*General Harry Crerar.*

General Arthur Grassett, a Canadian in the British army who was the General Officer Commanding of the garrison at Hong Kong at the beginning of the war, retired in July 1941. On his way back to England he went through Canada where he met in Ottawa with his old friend General Harry Crerar, Canada's Chief of General Staff. Grassett persuaded Crerar that Churchill was wrong, that Hong Kong could be defended with an additional two battalions of Canadian infantry. Just how far off the mark Grassett was in his assessment is made clear by his report to British High Command in Singapore a few months before he left the colony. Grassett wrote:

*Hong Kong is impregnable, and the Japanese have not the audacity or the capacity to attack us.*

After Grassett returned to England, and despite Churchill's warning, he managed to convince British High

Command that Hong Kong could indeed be defended against a Japanese attack, given two additional regiments. He also informed his superiors that he had it on good authority, despite Prime Minister Mackenzie King's earlier objections, that, if asked, Canada would be willing to comply with a request for troops.

The British High Command, on hearing these views and receiving Grassett's assurances that Canada would agree to supply troops, again raised the issue of reinforcing Hong Kong with Prime Minister Churchill. Churchill, I surmise, ever since he had heard Mackenzie King praise Hitler after his visit to Germany in 1937, had little time for King and his opinions. While I have found no supporting evidence, I believe that, faced with this renewed request, Churchill probably said, Mackenzie King was wrong about Hitler, and is wrong about reinforcing Hong Kong, but since they are his countrymen and I am in no position to argue, I will agree. In any event, on October 2, 1941, Churchill acquiesced to the Canadian reinforcement of Hong Kong.

All that could go wrong, had gone wrong in reaching this decision. But the die was cast. The British request was duly sent to Canada and, upon General Crerar's advice, finally accepted by a pressured and still reluctant, Mackenzie King.

Once the order was given, the regiments were selected in a great rush and the soldiers given short embarkation leaves to return home and say goodbye to their loved ones. They were given no idea of what was afoot, where they were going, or why. After traveling by train from Quebec and Manitoba, the Royal Rifles of Canada and the Winnipeg Grenadiers set sail from Vancouver aboard the troopship Awatea and the armed merchant cruiser Prince Robert on October 27, 1941.

As Murphy's Law would have it, "C-Force's" third vessel, containing its armoured vehicles, military transport, and certain types of ammunition, such as 5-inch mortar rounds, was delayed and eventually re-routed to Manila, its crucial cargo never to arrive and play a part in the battle. While the battle's outcome would be a foregone conclusion, the loss of this essential equipment, and especially of the mortar ammunition, made the mission even more difficult.

After the war, the Duff Commission's report to the government on the Hong Kong debacle generally whitewashed its causes. With respect to the missing transport ship, Mr. Justice Duff, a close friend of Mackenzie King, found that no one was really at fault. In the end, one or two headquarters officers received a reprimand for failing to dispatch the supply ship on time.

*Rt. Hon. Sir Lyman Poore Duff.*

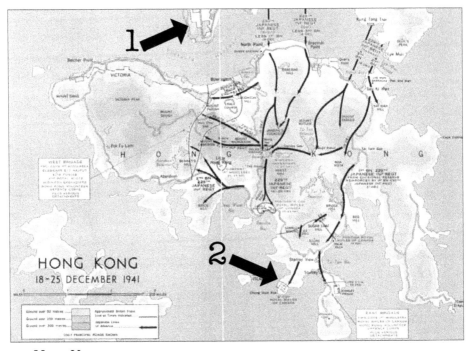

*Hong Kong*
*1) Kowloon*
*2) Stanley Peninsula*

CHAPTER 2

# The Battle of Hong Kong

Once in Hong Kong, the Canadians immediately began to explore the surroundings of their defense positions and to bolster them against attack.

Canadian morale was high. I can testify that we had great confidence in our officers and in our cause. Many of us were aware of our fathers' and uncles' brilliant record during World War I at Vimy Ridge and Amiens, and we knew of our regiments' sterling battle honours. We were determined, with the eyes of the world upon us, that no matter what happened, we would be a credit to our country. Not a negative word was heard about our situation. There was no complaining and no second guessing of our leadership. It was going to be tough. But we were determined to be up to the challenge, whatever it was.

At 8:00 a.m. on December 8, 1941, the Japanese struck without warning. The attack on Hong Kong was timed to coincide with the attack on the American naval base at Pearl Harbor. Waves of Japanese bombers attacked the colony, destroying our tiny air force while it was still on the ground in a matter of minutes. Simultaneously, the Japanese army attacked the outer perimeter of the land-based defenses in the New Territories on the mainland north of the island. This heavy and skillfully-led ground attack forced the British, Indian and Canadian defenders to gradually retreat towards Victoria Harbour and Kowloon Bay until it was clear that holding the Japanese on the mainland was impossible. By the morning of December 13 all allied forces originally stationed in the New Territories had been withdrawn to the island. The Japanese had taken control of the Hong Kong mainland in only five days. On the first day of battle, J.L. Ralston, Minister of National Defense, whose wish for Canadians to see battle had now been granted, cabled to Brigadier Lawson:

*Concurrently with the Dominion's declaration of war against Japan, I send you the assurance of complete confidence that the forces under your command will, in the days that lie ahead, worthily uphold the best traditions of Canadian Arms.*

The day of the retreat to the island, a document signed by Japanese General Sakai and sent across the harbour under a flag of truce requested the defenders to surrender to save further bloodshed, a request categorically refused by the British Governor, Sir Mark Young. Now the enemy began to shell, bomb and mortar our coastal defense works and to pound our defensive concrete pillboxes to rubble. The Lye Mun defense area closest to the mainland was especially subjected to a fierce and continual bombardment.

At 9:30 a.m. on December 17, General Sakai sent another white flag of truce across the water with second request for the colony to surrender. Again, the Japanese offer was rejected. The Japanese, when they considered our positions and our options, expressed surprise at our stubbornness.

At 10:30 p.m. on December 18, under a dense smoke

screen caused by a refinery fire, the Japanese began to land in great force at locations on the northeast side of the island. Despite heavy casualties, the Japanese poured ashore and in a few hours during the night of December 18-19 overran the Rajput defenders in fierce fighting, killing most of their officers and virtually wiping out the regiment. Next, they attacked and overran the Canadian defenders at Lye Mun, inflicting heavy casualties and by sheer weight of numbers infiltrating and penetrating our prepared lines of defense. Japanese intelligence was excellent, down to copies of British military maps of the island and its defense positions found on dead Japanese officers.

*Brigadier Lawson, C-Force Commander*

In the midst of the battle, Brigadier Lawson received a second cable, this one from Prime Minster MacKenzie King, who wrote:

*All Canada has been following hour by hour the progress of events in Hong Kong. Our thoughts are of each and every one of you in your brave resistance to the forces that are seeking to destroy the world's freedom. Your bravery is an inspiration to us all. Our country's name and its honour have never been more splendidly upheld.*

After their first lodgement on the island via Kowloon

Bay, Japanese reinforcements came ashore in successive waves and began to rapidly ascend the high ground, killing and driving back any defenders who stood in their way. During this thrust to secure the high ground in the centre of the island, the Japanese broke through to West Brigade headquarters at Wong Nei Chong Gap, commanded by Brigadier Lawson. His pillbox surrounded and receiving direct fire through its apertures, Lawson made a last phone call to east brigade headquarters to say that he and his staff were going outside to fight it out. The Brigadier and his entire staff died in the ensuing fight, except for one captain who was badly wounded and left for dead.

Canadian communications were now severed, and the island's defenders cut in two by powerful Japanese forces which now controlled the high ground and began to increase their advantage with more reinforcements. This violent thrust of the Japanese, under cover of the night, forced a contraction of the Canadian lines to a wide semi-circle in front of the Stanley Peninsula in the south of the island, making the peaks overlooking the peninsula the battleground for the opposing forces.

Commencing on the morning of the December 20, the Royal Rifles attempted again and again, in broad daylight and without any supporting mortar or artillery fire, to counterattack the Japanese positions atop the prominent mountain peaks of Sugar Loaf Hill, Boa Vista, Notting Hill, Bridge Hill, Red Hill, Brick Hill, Violet Hill and Stanley Mound. The attacks entailed scaling these heights in company strength through thick, entangling scrub and in the face of grenades and incessant enemy machine gun and mortar fire from above. Even under these horrific conditions our attacks were successful. But every time we finally reached a peak and drove the Japanese off, we were out of water, had no food, little ammunition and were nearly dead from the exhaustion from the day-long climb and fight in excruciating heat.

Colonel Stacey, in his *History of the Canadian Army in World War II*, states that in no other theatre of operations did Canadians face such steep and rugged terrain or suffer so much from battling on difficult ground. Simply to climb up these steep, tangled, scrub-covered slopes, loaded down with weapons, water and ammunition, was a major effort in itself. To do it all day, day after day, in attacks against a determined, well-led enemy who had to be killed to be evicted, ended in mind-numbing exhaustion. Keeping men and units together in some form of order and evacuating the wounded under these conditions was a nightmare. The undergrowth was so thick and the slopes so steep that many of the wounded were never found and died where they fell, at the bottom of some tangled ravine or scrub-covered fissure.

Our successes were short-lived. As soon as it became dark, fresh Japanese troops would mount an attack to regain any ground we had taken from them during the day. Under pressure from these attacks and now with no food, water, grenades and little ammunition, we were forced down the mountain with the wounded who could still walk, and those we could carry, to find ourselves at midnight, utterly spent, back at our starting point.

When dawn broke, as soon as water and food (bully beef and biscuits) and ammunition were brought up, the men were wakened and we would again be ordered to attack, each time within a smaller perimeter and each time with fewer men. The utter futility and agony of these attacks have haunted my dreams to this day. The Japanese outnumbered us by a substantial margin. They were well-led, veteran troops. When we stopped them in some position, because of their superior numbers they would immediately and skillfully begin to slip around us to turn our flanks, until, to avoid encirclement, we were forced to give ground and reduce our perimeter yet again. They were equipped with mobile mountain batteries and mortars, which were transported by mules. Their mountain battery equipment and mule transport in this mountainous terrain gave them an enormous advantage. They were superb at camouflage and field craft and their organization and fire discipline were excellent.

It was obvious that the British propaganda stating the Japanese were inferior troops was utterly false. Brigadier John Masters of the British Army who fought for months against the Japanese in the Burma Campaign had this to say about the Japanese as an enemy:

*They are the bravest people I have ever met. In our armies, any of them, nearly every Japanese would have a Congressional Medal of Honour or a Victoria Cross. It is the fashion to dismiss their courage as fanaticism but this only begs the question. They believed in something and they were willing to die for it...what else is bravery? They pressed home their attacks when no other troops would have done so....The Japanese simply came on using all their skill and rage until they were stopped by death. In defense, they held their ground with a furious tenacity that never faltered. They had to be killed company by company, squad by squad, man by man, to the last...*

But no less brave and steadfast were the battered and exhausted Canadian defenders of Hong Kong, as I can attest. Never did I see or hear of a single Canadian soldier who failed to carry out his orders, whether they were to hold fast or to attack. The culmination of this tenacious and determined resistance came on Christmas Day, the eighteenth day of continuous fighting, when the Japanese had almost completely overrun Hong Kong's defenses and we, the Royal Rifles, had been driven back and were stationed at the last stronghold of Stanley Fortress, at the south end of Stanley Peninsula with our backs to the sea.

Facing us, a half of a kilometre to the north, was Stanley Village, now occupied by the Japanese. We knew the end was near. We knew the blood lust of our enemy, we knew that tomorrow or the day after, our young lives would come to a grisly end.

Here is the story of the last battle of Hong Kong.

Early on Christmas morning I was awakened and summoned to a meeting with Lieutenant Powers and Major Parker, my Company Commander. We were told that our British Brigade Commander, Brigadier Wallis, had ordered us to attack Stanley Village, clear it of the enemy, and occupy and hold a series of bungalows on a ridge near the centre of the village. The attack was to commence at 1 p.m. I would command one half of D company, Lieutenant Powers the other half. There would be no artillery or machine gun support.

To attempt this attack in broad daylight, with our exhausted troops, without covering fire, over the open ground in front of the village, was preposterous. In the words of a British artillery officer who witnessed this action:

*The Canadian attack on the Stanley Village was suicidal.*

Military historian Carl Vincent agreed. In No Reason Why, his study of the Battle of Hong Kong, Vincent states:

*This attack for idiotic futility, ranks with the charge of the Light Brigade.*

I knew when I heard our orders that my luck had finally run out. Christmas Day 1941 was to be my last day on earth. As I proceeded back to my men, I wondered how they would react to the mission.

I assembled them and gave them their orders for the

33

attack. There was complete silence as they stared at me with incredulous eyes. As the fateful orders sank in not one of these battle-stained, exhausted men spoke, not one moved. The silence was complete.

I made a short speech. Since we had no thought of surrender, I said, then taking part in this attack was really no worse than staying where we were to await our deaths in a final, overwhelming Japanese attack on our position. I told them how proud I was of their conduct on the battlefield to this moment, how they had never flinched, never failed to do their duty, and how they had upheld the honour of our regiment and our country.

Then I said, "Let's go down into that village, carry out our orders, do our best, and show Major Parker what we can do."

Numbering 120 men when the Japanese attacked on December 8, D Company was down to a little over 70 effectives by December 25. Since two of my corporal section leaders had recently been killed, I appointed two riflemen, one of whom was Rifleman Charlie MacLean, as new section leaders, and organized my stripped down force into attack formations. We began to clean our weapons, stock up on water, ammunition and grenades. Then I told my men to rest and try to sleep until I called them, close to our start time. Not a single rifleman asked to be excused or showed any outward sign of distress. Every man who could stand and use a weapon was prepared to go, without exception. As always, they planned to go as a team, a team assembled from the cities, towns, small villages and the farms of eastern Canada where they had grown up together, volunteered together, trained, gone on leave, laughed, cried and partied together. This was a band of brothers who never let their comrades down, a brotherhood where duty was never shirked.

I will never forget my feelings on that Christmas

morning, 72 years ago. I was proud to be the leader of these men and fearful of what might happen that afternoon. I cannot remember being personally afraid, only fearful of failing in my responsibility as a leader. And I was preoccupied before the attack - studying map references to pinpoint our start line, plotting the attack route and memorizing the details of Stanley Village, our objective. I also had to arrange for stretchers to evacuate the wounded, ensure that automatic weapons, ammunition, grenades, and water were properly allocated to each of our sections, and ensure all was ready to go by 1 p.m.

Timing was important. Since my own watch had been broken, Lester Sauson, one of my fellow sergeants, lent me his.

Zero hour arrived. We formed up and split into our two attack groups, one under my command, the other under Lieutenant Powers, and headed down through the rocks and scrub towards our the start line. This line was just below and slightly east of the large cemetery lying between us and our village objective and roughly in line with Stanley Prison, now one of our forward positions. My group moved forward just west of the prison, Lieutenant Powers' group just east of it. Despite the cover, our early movements were detected and drew mortar and machine gun fire from the Japanese entrenched and sheltered by the gravestones and monuments in the cemetery 250 metres ahead of us.

By sprints and crawls, dodging from rock to rock and tree to tree, we made our way to the start line, thankfully with only one serious casualty in my group to that point. On the other side of Stanley Prison, a hundred metres to our right, Lieutenant Powers and his group also reached their start position on schedule, his force intact. But I could see we were all too exposed to suffer delay and hastily arranged my men in a single attack line, ordered them to fix bayonets, then yelled the order – loud enough for

Lieutenant Powers and his men to hear me - to charge the graveyard.

We started at the run, my men spread out on either side of me, and with fearsome war whoops rushed the enemy across 200 metres of open ground, firing from the hip, heaving grenades, and soon dodging grave stones as we ran. Within seconds, a violent melee erupted as combatants clashed in the cemetery. The enemy, sudden looming figures in green camouflage uniforms and bell-shaped helmets, rose to meet us, bayonets fixed, and fierce, chaotic hand-to-hand struggles took place among the graves.

It was at this moment I very nearly lost my life when a Japanese soldier sprang suddenly from behind a gravestone and lunged at me with his bayonet. I dodged the blade and I clamped the end of his rifle in the crook of my left arm, and held it against my body. As he started trying to withdraw it, cutting my arm with his bayonet as he pulled, Charlie MacLean, who was right behind me, intervened and dispatched the enemy.

Powered by a fierce momentum to break on through, our wild assault was unstoppable. The Japanese soon broke and ran in terror, my men right behind them, firing into their retreating backs. By now the ground was littered with dead and wounded, most of them Japanese. They ran for cover in the first house above and just outside the far side of the cemetery, with us still hot on their heels. We quickly surrounded the house and evicted the Japanese, room by room, using grenades and bayonets.

With that first house cleared of the enemy, we continued on towards the village with little or no resistance until suddenly all firing stopped and we seemed to be in the clear. At this point I called a halt behind a hedge that gave us some cover. We caught our breath, reloaded our weapons and, because of our casualties, re-balanced our formations.

This pause lasted a minute or so. Peeking through the

hedge we saw a platoon of 30 to 35 Japanese reinforcements trotting silently behind their officer toward us. They were closed up in a double file with their rifles at the trail and completely unaware of our presence.

We waited until they were nearly upon us then stepped into the open with our automatics blazing. In less than a minute they were mowed down almost where they stood. As those at the front collapsed about a half a dozen at the rear of their column broke in panic and ran into a driveway sloping toward a nearby house. They were killed before they got off a shot.

Again at the run, we headed for the bungalows on the ridge that were our final objective. They were lightly occupied and resistance was soon overcome. At this point, I was joined by the other half of the company, now under the command of Sergeant Lance Ross, who informed me that Lieutenant Powers had been badly wounded in the legs by machine gun bullets during the attack.

We took up positions inside and along side the bungalows and prepared for the inevitable counterattack. By this time I had lost a lot of men, but we had managed to hold onto most of our automatic weapons. Sergeant Ross and I had just enough time to position our men and our Bren guns before the Japanese came at us across the open ground in front of us. We were ready, and poured withering fire into our attackers. After suffering terrible casualties, their counterattack stalled, just as their artillery began registering on our bungalows.

By now I had lost all sense of time and have no idea how long this deafening stalemate lasted. But as the Japanese ground attack diminished, their artillery found the range. Exploding shells began to shoot our bungalows to pieces, blowing out the roofs and front walls of our positions. My force was now greatly reduced in numbers, out of water, with only two or three grenades left and running short of ammunition.

At this point, a dispatch runner made it through the mayhem with a message from Major Parker, who was observing the action from the high ground behind us. His message said that the enemy was encircling our left flank to cut us off and ordered me to withdraw with my men as quickly as possible. After a huddle with Sergeant Ross I ordered our remaining section leaders to carry out the retreat by leading our survivors back through the cemetery in groups of two or three. Once they were south of the cemetery and across the open ground beyond they were to establish a defensive line in front of Stanley Prison. Off they went in staggered groups and while the withdrawal took place Sergeant Ross and I kept up covering fire from our Bren gun positions in the bungalows. The ground before us was littered with dead Japanese. Now, almost out of ammunition and with our men gone, Ross and I began leap-frogging back towards our lines, covering each other with Bren gun fire as we retreated. We finally got far enough back to drop our heavy weapons and run for a drainage ditch that seemed to lead to safety.

No such luck. The advancing Japanese quickly mounted a nambu machine gun aimed directly at our ditch and we were immediately pinned down in a hail of fire. The ditch was deep enough to give us a moment's breather but as we turned to get our bearings we could see the far side of the ditch being torn up by bullets that were skimming over us by only two or three inches. A slight drop in the gun's firing angle and we were goners: we had to make a break for it. And it was then, for a split second as I lay glued to the ditch's slope with my arms stretched out in front of me with bullets whining overhead, that I noticed Sergeant Sauson's watch on my wrist and felt a sudden pang: by the look of things he was never going to get it back!

Suddenly the firing stopped and we grabbed our chance.

As the Japanese gunner was reloading the machine gun with a new magazine we vaulted out of the far side of the ditch and sprinted towards Stanley Prison. We were now on open ground with 150 metres to cover before we reached safety. When the machine gun opened up again we were only halfway there, so we zig-zagged and dove behind the only protection near us, a big, black Bentley sedan that had been disabled and abandoned earlier in the battle.

Now the intense machine gun fire homed in on the hulk of the car. As we crouched behind the quickly disintegrating wreck, bullets riddled the doors, deflated the tires, shattering glass and metal alike. That poor old Bentley could only take so much and when the gunner paused to reload again we made a final mad dash for the safety of our lines at Stanley Prison, and made it.

Finally out of the line of fire, Ross and I, bloody, filthy and exhausted, began to look for our troops. As the sun was setting, we were met by Major Parker, our commanding officer, beside the trail.

"Are you the last?" Parker asked.

"Yes sir, we are," I replied.

He bowed his head and said, "My God, my God," as tears streamed down his cheeks. Out of more than 70 men, only 44 members of D Company had made it back. Ross and I were numbers 45 and 46.

*Major Maurice A. Parker, Company Commander "D" Coy., Royal Rifles.*

Twenty-six of my men had died in that gallant but pointless attack on Stanley Village.

A few hours later, sometime after eight o'clock in the evening of that grim Christmas Day, we were ordered to lay down our arms. We were told that Governor Mark Young had surrendered to the Japanese and hostilities had ceased.

The Battle of Hong Kong was over.

*Epilogue*

We slept the night of the surrender in Stanley Fortress. When we awoke the next day, we found the Japanese had pulled back out of sight. All was quiet. The following day, I asked for permission to take a small group of men back to Stanley Village to find and bury our dead. I led my party north, armed with shovels, until I met a Japanese sentry. After negotiating with a Japanese officer, who could speak English, we were allowed to carry on with our mission.

As we proceeded into the village, we could see the Japanese fires and row after row of their dead waiting to be cremated, the ashes to be returned, as was their custom, in little white containers to Japan. At the site where we had confronted the Japanese reinforcement platoon, the ditches on both sides of the road were blackened with their dried blood. Our mission objective, the bungalows on the ridge of the village, had been badly damaged by the Japanese artillery bombardment. Here it seemed strangely quiet.

We buried our dead where we found them. As each of our men was committed to his shallow grave, we bowed our heads and I said a soldier's farewell prayer for each. One of them was rifleman and acting corporal Charlie MacLean, the man whose quick action had saved my life. He was hit by machine gun fire as we were entering the village, was badly wounded and died a brave death in the bungalow we reached together.

Sergeant Lester Sauson got his watch back. He became a prisoner of war after the surrender of Hong Kong and in the spring of 1943 was one of 300 prisoners shipped to Niigata on the Sea of Japan to work as slave labour at the Rinko Coal Company. On the night of December 31, 1943, the roof of a poorly constructed barracks in Niigata Camp 5 collapsed under the weight of snow. About 150 prisoners were sleeping inside. Lester Sauson and seven others were killed by the falling beams and debris.

CHAPTER 3

# Prisoners of War

The Canadians of "C-Force" in the 18 day Battle of Hong Kong suffered 783 casualties. For those who survived the fighting, nearly four years of starvation, slave labour, and brutal abuse now began.

As examples of the captive experience under the Japanese, here are excerpts from the diary of Sergeant Lance Ross of the Royal Rifles, excerpts from the confidential medical report of Captain Stanley Banfill, a Royal Rifles Medical Officer, and excerpts from the findings of the International War Crimes Tribunal for the Far East in its report published in 1948.

Sergeant Lance Ross:

*Jan 2, 1942: Very fine day. The stench is terrible. We put ground over some of the bodies.*
*Feb 13: We are almost frozen and our roof leaks awful.*
*Feb 16: Dysentery is widespread throughout the camp.*
*Feb 18: I believe we are going to starve to death.*
*Feb 22: We are terribly hungry. Just talk about food.*

*March 1: We are getting lousy as coots. We are crowded so close together.*

*March 23: Rice and water 3 times a day.*

*April 20: Hitler's birthday, also Aunt Bessie's. Many more to her.*

*May 14: Japanese knocked out a Chinese and left him on the street (outside the camp) in rain all day. Just before dark bayoneted him; he was alive this morning.*

*May 16: Japanese have two Chinese women tied to a post. They have shot their husbands.*

*May 25: Heat getting bad, 110 degrees (45' C) in shade. Mosquitoes eating us alive.*

*June 13: Japanese say they attacked Aleutians. Bedbugs getting worse.*

*June 30: Food is awful. Rice in morning - bun dinner - some kind of greens like weeds.*

*July 14: Heavy rain all night. Sleep outdoors on concrete so many bugs.*

*Aug 12: Man died. Many going blind - gradually getting weaker.*

*Aug 16: Conditions getting unbearable, we will all die in this terrible place.*

*Aug 27: Hot, 100 degrees (35' C) in shade. Two men died last night.*

*Sept 1: Rain and mud. First man of my section died with dysentery.*

*Sept 11: More men falling sick every day.*

*Sept 12: Another died today, we wrapped him in a sheet, buried him across the road.*

*Sept 14: Another death in my platoon, pneumonia.*

*Sept 19: Very hot. Men dying at rate of three a day, malaria, dysentery, fever.*

*Sept 21: More sick, some going blind. 3 died today.*

Captain Stanley Banfill, Medical Officer of the Royal Rifles:

*The first four months after our move [to Sham Shui Po POW camp] - September '42 to January '43 - were the most difficult and depressing of our imprisonment. I think the chief factors that made this so were forced labour, malnutrition and the diphtheria epidemic.*

*The Japanese were engaged in clearing away the debris of war and were lengthening the landing strip at Kai Tak....The Japanese demanded a certain number of men each day and set the quota high. Eventually it became clear even to our captors that they were asking the impossible of sick and exhausted men and the work parties were discontinued.*

*The food was inadequate in both amount and kind. Rice and greens ("green horror") with hardly any fats and an occasional minute ration of fish was near starvation to us. As a result we developed severe malnutrition and this aggravated the tropical diseases and those spread by our crowding that now hit us....*

*The result was disastrous as 74 Canadians developed diphtheria before we could get any antitoxin and, of these, 54 died. When we started having several deaths a day the Japanese became alarmed. Possibly the disease was spreading to their troops and their seniors demanded action. They began swabbing throats to detect carriers and insisted everyone on pain of punishment wear a face mask day and night.*

*They showed their fear of criticism by ordering that diphtheria should not appear as the cause of death on our reports and, most surprising, Dr. Saito [chief medical officer for all Hong Kong POW camps] lined up all medical personnel, mostly devoted volunteer orderlies, and slapped their faces for permitting their patients to die....Our physical ailments were mostly due to malnutrition and could only have been treated adequately with good food. We had every known deficiency disease except scurvy. Everyone suffered from some degree of beriberi and pellagra and we saw all of their unpleasant manifestations - the severe sleep robbing pain of "hot foot" was almost unbearable to the victim and increasing, and sometimes sudden, blindness seemed to forecast a hopeless future. We also had the common tropical diseases whose effect was exaggerated in men suffering from malnutrition....Tropical ulcers were common and parasitic infestation was universal.*

## The 1948 Report of the International War Crimes Tribunal for the Far East:

*The evidence relating to atrocities and other conventional war crimes presented before the Tribunal establishes that from the opening of the war in China until the surrender of Japan in 1945 torture, murder and rape and other cruelties of the most inhumane and barbarous character were freely practised by the Japanese army and navy. During a period of several months, the Tribunal heard evidence, orally or by affidavit, from witnesses who testified in detail to atrocities committed in all theatres of war on a scale so vast, yet following so common a pattern in all theatres, that only one conclusion is possible – the atrocities were either secretly ordered or willfully permitted by the Japanese Government or individual members thereof and by the leaders of the armed forces....*

*From beginning to end, the customary and conventional rules of war designed to prevent inhumanity were flagrantly disregarded. Ruthless killing of prisoners by shooting, decapitation, drowning and other methods; death marches in which prisoners including the sick were forced to march long distances under conditions which not even*

*War Crimes Tribunal for the Far East, Tokyo.*

*well-conditioned troops could stand, many of those dropping out or bayoneted by guards; forced labour in tropical heat without protection from the sun; complete lack of housing and medical supplies in many cases, resulting in thousands of deaths from disease; beatings and torture of all kinds to extract information as confessions or for minor offenses; killing without trial of recaptured prisoners after escape and for attempting to escape; killing without trial of captured aviators; and even cannibalism: these are some of the atrocities of which proof was made before the Tribunal.*

Immediately after the war, this military tribunal found guilty and executed 920 Japanese for war crimes that even included cannibalism of Allied soldiers. Most of them were Japanese officers, and three of them - Tojo, Yamashita and Homma - were the most high-ranking Japanese generals. Among other crimes, Colonel Isao Tokunaga, the senior

General Tojo,
Japanese Minister for war.

General Yamashita.

47

officer in command of all Prisoners of War at Hong Kong, was sentenced to death for the murder of four Canadian and five British prisoners of war following his trial for war crimes against Canadian and British internees at Hong Kong

Prisoners lived in constant anxiety on a day-to-day basis and in fear of what next act of unpremeditated violence and sadistic brutality would be their lot. But, as on the battlefield, the Canadians never gave up, never lost their belief in their cause and never lost their indomitable will to resist. Despite the beatings, the violence, and the daily attempts to cause fear and the complete humiliation of their prisoners, the Japanese failed in their mission to break their morale. The Canadian spirit was never broken. And while they had lost the battle of Hong Kong, the soldiers of the Royal Rifles of Canada and the Winnipeg Grenadiers never lost their self respect, their patriotism, or the mettle of which they were made.

In the chapters that follow I will tell you about some of these Canadian soldiers whose resistance and sabotage was beyond the normal call of duty and bounds of courage.

*General Homma.*

*Col. Tokunaga,*
*P.O.W. Commandant, Hong Kong.*

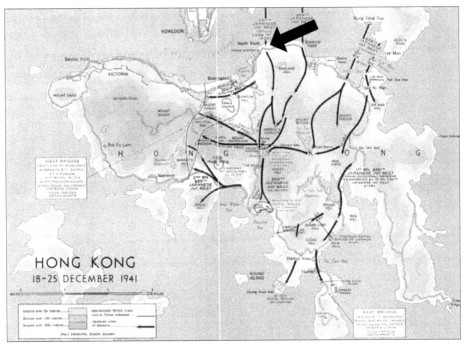

North Point Prison Camp, Hong Kong.

CHAPTER 4

# The Escapers

After the Governor surrendered Hong Kong on Christmas Day and ordered the allies to lay down their arms, both sides began to tend to their dead.

On the fifth day after the surrender the Japanese began to march the Canadian survivors across the island to North Point, on the opposite side of the island. Here they had prepared a prison camp for us which before the war had been a Chinese refugee camp. This camp was for Canadians only. British prisoners were sent to Sham Shui Po on the mainland.

North Point Camp, where the Japanese had initially landed, had been a fierce battleground and was littered with the dead and decomposing bodies of men and pack animals. The litter, filth and stench of the dead were awful, and a perfect breeding ground for millions of flies. The huts were riddled with shrapnel, and there was no running water, no latrines, no cooking facilities and no food or water for the prisoners. The ground was ploughed up by shellfire and covered with the wreckage of the battle.

Upon arrival, the men, many of them walking wounded

*North Point Prison Camp, Hong Kong.*

and all of them exhausted, simply lay on the ground or on the cement floor of the shattered, windowless huts. The crowding of the facilities, such as they were, made for hopeless congestion. Lice, fleas and bedbugs were rampant. There was no soap and not even simple items of hygiene, such as toothbrushes, were available.

The men were filthy and battle-stained. Within a short time many were infected by the clouds of disease-carrying flies and began succumbing to a virulent form of amoebic dysentery. There were no medical supplies, no hospital, and no provisions for the sick and the wounded. The seriously wounded and the dysentery cases lay on their stretchers where we had set them down. They were now covered with their own blood and filth and crawling with flies. This was our introduction to a Japanese camp and to how the Japanese treated their prisoners.

When food was finally issued the day after our arrival, it

*North Point Prison Camp, Hong Kong.*

consisted of mouldy rice full of rat droppings and worms. Our rations were two bowls of rice per day, one in the morning and one in the evening, and one sourdough bun per man, at noon. Nutritionists have calculated that in order to maintain health and weight, a soldier or an average male engaged in manual labour requires 3,500 calories per day. It is estimated that at North Point Camp, where the diet consisted almost entirely of rice and chrysanthemum tops, the caloric intake for the individual prisoner was about 1,200 calories per day. Along with the lack of calories in the daily diet was the severe deficiency of essential vitamins such as B complex, so essential to maintaining health. Even after battlefield experience, these shocking conditions were hard to believe. Nonetheless, as we settled into these conditions we assessed our situation and came to a collective determination:

*We may have lost a battle, but we have not lost the war! We are still members of the Canadian Army, who are only temporarily under Japanese control, and for us the war goes on. No matter how bad it gets, we will never give up and we will never fail to do our duty. Where it is at all possible we will carry out Churchill's last order "to maintain our resistance." We will never forget who we are and we will live up to our values and to our best traditions. As soldiers, we will see this thing through to the end, and we will live to have the last laugh!*

Sergeant John Payne,
Winnipeg Grenadiers.

One of those who believed strongly in this view was a handsome young man from Winnipeg, Manitoba, named John Oliver Payne. He was an artist, a musician and a typographer before he enlisted in the Winnipeg Grenadiers at the very beginning of the war. He was a leader and an exceptional soldier who, at age 23, had risen to the rank of sergeant in his regiment. Sergeant Payne knew it was our duty to escape. Because of the deliberate Japanese refusal to release information to any news source he was aware that no one in Canada knew what had happened to "C-Force" at Hong Kong. As far as Canadians were concerned nearly two thousand men had disappeared without a trace. Payne believed that someone had to escape to report on the military situation to Army Headquarters in Ottawa. He also understood the importance of explaining first-hand to the fearful and increasingly anxious families as well as the Canadian public what had happened to their soldiers and family members. And he knew that given the starvation diet at North Point Camp he would have to escape soon, before he became physically incapable of making the attempt. Supported by his officers, it was in these pressing circumstances that Sergeant Payne volunteered to lead an escape attempt to inform the outside world of "C Force's" fate. His destination was the Chinese capital of Chunking (today Chongqing) in south-west China. His party would be limited to four, the other three escapees chosen by lot from the many fellow soldiers willing to join his dangerous mission.

To escape from the island of Hong Kong was a daunting task. Not only was it surrounded by water, but four caucasians, once outside the wire, would stand out among the Chinese population. As well, neither Payne nor his comrades could speak Chinese and the Canadian POWs had no Chinese helpers or contacts outside the wire. Little though we had, camp resources were pooled to provide Payne and his party with the best boots, socks, and clothing available, as well as maps, a compass and extra rations. They were also issued with a knife and a revolver that had been smuggled in and hidden in the camp.

As escape plans crystalized, conditions in North Point Prison Camp worsened. Japanese brutality was a constant occurrence. The starvation diet and unsanitary conditions led to skyrocketing disease among the prisoners, and for some to death. Payne weighed the odds and the reasons for his attempt. Even if they were lucky enough to reach the mainland, they still had a trip of more than 1,800 kilometres to Chunking, some of it through Japanese-controlled territory. It was a monumental challenge. But Payne is said to have reflected that while he knew the escape risks were high, he thought the chances of surviving the conditions in North Point Prison Camp were almost on par. And as well as the compelling need to alert allied authorities of the appalling conditions of the POWs at North Point Camp and the circumstances of other allied prisoners and captured Hong Kong civilians, Payne also believed that escape must be attempted for its own sake. Fighting back however one could was a soldier's duty.

*Lance-Corporal George Berzenski, Winnipeg Grenadiers.*

On August 19, 1942, eight months after the fall of Hong Kong, Sergeant John Payne, Lance-Corporal George Berzenski, Private John Adams, and Private Percy Ellis were ready. During a rain storm the following night, the four brave Grenadiers made their escape using a bamboo ladder to scale the electrified barbed wire fence. It was the last we saw of them. We learned later, from unofficial Japanese sources, that Payne and his men stole a sampan and were halfway across Hong Kong harbour when it sank. They swam for the mainland, but before reaching shore they were discovered by a Japanese patrol boat and taken into custody. Transported to Stanley prison, the four were tortured by the Kempeitai or Japanese Military Police - sadistic thugs roughly equivalent to the Nazi Gestapo - who tried to force them to reveal their escape supporters in

*Private John Adams,*
*Winnipeg Grenadiers.*

*Private Percy Ellis,*
*Winnipeg Grenadiers.*

North Point Camp. Never breaking under torture, the four refused to implicate their comrades. Sometime in October, according to Chinese witnesses, the end came when they were executed by firing squad. The execution took place at King's Park football field in Hong Kong.

The day before their escape, Sergeant Payne wrote a last letter to his mother. Captured in its loving, light-hearted words are the spirit, gallant humour and unflinching sense of duty that John Payne, George Berzenski, John Adams and Percy Ellis embodied as they jumped the prison fence and disappeared into the night on a mission in which they had slimmest chance of survival:

*Dear Mater,*

*I have decided, either fortunately or unfortunately as the case may be, to take a chance on getting through to Chunking. I've investigated as much as possible and feel sure we stand a jolly good chance of getting there. There are numerous reasons for this step, the chief being that the cholera season and fly season is starting, dysentery and beriberi are high in camp, and anyway I'm ruddy sick of Japanese hospitality.*

*You share, I know, my own views on fatalism, so for that reason I know you won't condemn my judgment. So just in case I shouldn't make it, you must remember that according to our beliefs I have departed for a much nicer place (I hope), although it will grieve me to exchange the guitar for a harp, even though there is a higher percentage of gold in the latter. But that's enough of this drivel, I'll be able to destroy this note myself, I'm sure, so bye-bye for now...*

*Your devoted son,*

*John*

*P.S. Best regards to Di & Yvonne.*

*Tell Ben to join the Air Force next war.*

For their brave attempt Sergeant Payne, Lance Corporal Berzenski, and privates Adams and Ellis, were all awarded a "Mentioned in Despatches."

*Mentioned in Despatches Oak Leaf.*

Sergeant Payne's gravestone at Sai Wan War Cemetry reads;
     Put to death by the Enemy
   "His spirit must be our banner"

*Graves for Private John Adams, Lance-Corporal George Berzenski, Private Percy Ellis and Sergeant John Payne, Sai Wan War Cemetry, Hong Kong.*

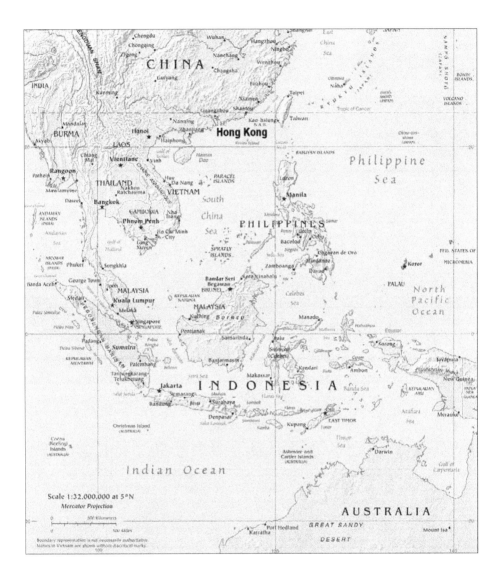

CHAPTER 5

# The Plotters

In March 1942, almost immediately after his capture and imprisonment at Hong Kong, Major J.D. Clague of the British army made a daring escape from Sham Shui Po Prison Camp on the Chinese mainland. He had discovered a drain unknown to his captors that lay deep beneath the camp and emptied into Victoria Harbour. Making his way through this drain, he dove in the water and swam ashore some distance from the camp. A series of hair-raising experiences followed, but his fluency in Chinese and his long experience with the Chinese, who assisted and guided him, allowed him to avoid Japanese patrols. After weeks of dangerous travel Clague managed to reach the American air base in China at Kweilin (Guilin), more than 500 kilometres to the north-west.

From China he was immediately flown to London to report to Brigadier Norman Crockett. Crockett was commander of a secret British special forces unit whose job was to establish contact and liaison with allied prisoners of war, to gather information, and to help prisoners escape wherever they were held.

After listening to Clague's report and assessing the situation in China, Crockett decided that Clague's language skills and his knowledge of the Hong Kong situation made him the ideal person to send back to China to enlist members of the Chinese guerrilla army to help effect a mass escape of allied prisoners from the camps at Hong Kong.

Major Clague, who had a taste for cloak and dagger work, returned to China in the late spring of 1942 under the code name "Iron Foot" and set up headquarters at Waichow in a remote part of Kwangchung Province, some 60 miles from Hong Kong. His first step was to recruit Chinese guerillas to pose as foremen and infiltrate the POW work gangs which the Japanese has begun using as slave labour to rebuild Kai Tak airport. Once Clague established communication with the prisoners, planning for a breakout could begin.

There were two prison camps in Hong Kong by this time, both in Kowloon, on the mainland. The more populous camp was Sham Shui Po, which held British and Canadian other ranks. Argyle, a much smaller camp, was for officers only. The camps lay about four miles apart and were allowed absolutely no contact with one another. Clague learned that the senior British officer at Sham Shui Po was a remarkable 25-year-old Captain of the Royal Scots named Douglas Ford.

*Major J.D.Clague "Iron Foot."*

Clague began sending messages to Ford, passed by his Chinese operatives working as foremen to allied POWs from Sham Shui Po assigned to the Kai Tak work site, requesting that a liaison be set up

*Sham Shui Po prison camp.*

between Ford and "Iron Foot". This was a risky business right under the noses of the Japanese guards and, at first, Ford feared a Japanese trap. But eventually, after analyzing Clague's handwriting and other details, Ford established the bona fides of "Iron Foot" and sent a reply to Waichow.

With communication established, Major Clague began sending escape maps, compasses and life-saving medicines and diphtheria serum which were smuggled into Sham Shui Po

*Captain Douglas Ford, Royal Scots.*

through the clandestine pipeline Clague and Ford carefully set up. The method used to smuggle items into the camps and send messages out was to conceal the contraband among the supplies and goods containers that were shipped to the camps on ration trucks from a wide variety of supply points once or twice a week. This necessitated the involvement of Sergeants Hardy and Farrel, two British POWs working as lorry drivers, as well as two Chinese civilian volunteers. These brave men knew all too well what would happen if they were caught.

It was at this stage that Lieutenant-Colonel John Price, commanding officer of the Royal Rifles and initially imprisoned at Argyle Camp, succeeded in his request to be transferred from Argyle to Sham Shui Po to be with his men. On arrival he became the senior allied officer in the camp. In handing over command, Captain Ford disclosed to Price the existence of the smuggling activity and the secret plans for a mass escape and asked Price to assume the command of the conspiracy as well. Price agreed.

In January 1943, soon after Colonel Price arrived at Sham Shui Po, the fragile network was disturbed when Sergeant Farrel was shipped on a work draft to Japan. Price then approached Ronald Routledge, a sergeant in the Royal Canadian Corps of Signals, to take Farrel's place as lorry driver, including his involvement in the dangerous

smuggling work. Routledge volunteered without hesitation and became a key player in the plot.

At Argyle Officers Camp, in the meantime, Colonel L.A. Newham of the British Army became head of Argyle's escape committee, with Flight Lieutenant Gray of the RAF as his assistant. Through Clague's

*Colonel L.A. Newham.* pipeline Newham and Gray

established a liaison with Price's plotters at Sham Shui Po. Now, as well as Colonel Price, even Maltby, the highest ranking British officer in the Hong Kong prison camps, was implicated in the plot and vulnerable to discovery.

By the spring of 1943 Colonel Price at Sham Shui Po, Colonel Newham at Argyle and Major Clague at Waichow were operating a triangular smuggling network supplied and controlled by Clague, as well as preparing a simultaneous and coordinated mass prison

*Sergeant Ronald Routledge,*
*Royal Canadian Corps of Signals.*

breakout from both camps, to be aided by Chinese guerrillas. The escape scheme was detailed and bold, including an air raid by allied planes as a diversion. This was a very dangerous undertaking requiring an audacious plan. Everyone involved knew that it was their duty to attempt to escape and the awful personal consequences if they were found out. The daily Japanese efforts to starve, humiliate, and destroy the prisoners' self respect, morale and loyalty to their cause only hardened the soldiers' resolve to escape, or at the very least to help others in the attempt.

Then disaster struck. Somehow, the link between Waichow and Argyle was compromised and on July 1, 1943, Colonel Newham was arrested at Argyle and Sergeant Routledge was arrested at Sham Shui Po. Both men were taken to Stanley Prison, the "Bastille" of Hong Kong, and

*Flight Lieutenant Gray.*

placed in solitary confinement. Shortly afterward, Captain Ford, Flight Lieutenant Gray, and Sergeant Hardy were also arrested and taken to Stanley Prison. From here on the five prisoners were under the brutal control of the Japanese Kempeitai who were determined to learn the names of everyone involved in the escape plot. The Kempeitai interrogators were especially anxious to have their prisoners implicate commanders such as General Maltby and Colonel Price so that an orgy of executions of senior officers could be justified.

Ford and Routledge were the first to be tortured. Other POWs in the prison, who were serving jail terms for lesser crimes, testified to the type and extent of the torture Ford and Routledge endured at the hands of the Kempeitai. From solitary confinement they would be dragged to a macabre torture chamber with its gruesome fittings of hosepipes, pliers, whips and wracks, its floor littered with bloodstained fingernails and broken teeth, where they were subjected to the barbarous application of these hideous devices. Week after week they suffered this vicious treatment. Each time, having given nothing but their name, rank and serial number, they were thrown back into their dark, damp, filthy cells where they lay twisted and bleeding on the stone floor without even a blanket to cover them. Through an endless fog of horror and pain the two brave men resisted every interrogation till they were mutilated almost beyond recovery and barely alive. Yet their answer to their sadistic interrogators was unwavering: name, rank and serial number, nothing more.

When the Kempeitai failed to break Ford and Routledge, they moved on to Colonel Newham and

Lieutenant Gray, only to be frustrated by the same stoic, heroic response of silence no matter what was suffered. Over nearly six months of this unspeakable brutality, the torturers learned nothing.

Proceedings then took a different turn. On December 1, 1943, Ford, Newham, Gray, Hardy and Routledge were placed on trial in a crude mockery of justice. They were charged with espionage, despite the fact that none of them had been engaged in a single act of espionage. They were simply carrying out their duty as soldiers to try to escape. Against these trumped up charges the Japanese court permitted no defense. No plea of innocence was allowed.

The three judges were Japanese officers, namely: Major-General Adache Shigero, Colonel Esao Tokunaga and Lieutenant Yamaguchi Kyoichi – all three of them perfect examples of the brutal Japanese military culture and the arrogant self-promotion of the Japanese Master Race. The prosecutor was Major Kogi Konuo, assisted by the chief executioner of the Stanley Jail.

Torture even stalked the courtroom. During the proceedings, the judges permitted the court interpreter to cut Colonel Newham's face to ribbons with a bamboo switch when he refused to incriminate any of his comrades. But their lust for blood came up short. Ford, in his flogged and

*Colonel Esao Tokunaga, Hong Kong.*

weakened state, now tried to take the lion's share of the blame, telling the court he was the ringleader of the smuggling operation and that Sergeants Routledge and Hardy, the NCO lorry drivers, were ignorant of the overall plot and were only carrying out his orders.

The judicial farce soon came to an end. Ford, Newham and Gray were sentenced to death, Routledge and Hardy to 15 years in prison.

Even on his way to execution Captain Ford tried to save his comrades by taking the blame, though to no avail. On December, 19, 1943, the three officers were executed on Cheko Wan Beach in Hong Kong, a beach where in better times Ford, the handsome young Scot from Edinburgh, had often gone swimming with his friends. Chinese witnesses say that as a final indignity, the Japanese ordered their mutilated victims to dig their own graves beside the three crosses already driven into the beach as markers of their execution. The men were by now physically incapable of such exertion so the Japanese lashed them to their crosses and lined up the firing squad. In a crash of gunfire on that bright December morning these brave soldiers finally made their escape - if not to their homes in Britain, at least to eternity.

*Epilogue*

In December 1943, Sergeant Routledge and Sergeant Hardy were sent to the horrible Japanese Military Prison at Canton to begin their prison terms. That was the last their fellow prisoners heard of them until after the Japanese surrender, almost two years later. It was then, immediately after his own release from Sham Shui Po in August 1945, that Colonel Price with great urgency sent a force of British Marines to discover the fate of his men at Canton. Bursting into the military prison, the marines, to their astonishment and delight, found both Sergeant Routledge and Sergeant Hardy still alive - bloodied, starving, near death, but unbowed.

Major C.R. Boxer, a British army officer and a fellow prisoner at the Canton Military Prison, later testified in a letter to Colonel Price concerning Sergeant Routledge's prison conduct:

*During the period of our incarceration, particularly the first six months when the whole party was fed on totally inadequate rations and subjected to severe disciplinary punishment with the object of undermining our health and morale, Sergeant Routledge remained unfailingly cheerful and resolute, giving an outstanding example of fortitude under exceptionally difficult conditions. He was at all times ready and willing to help the physically weaker members of the party and his careful and conscientious nursing of Sergeant Hardy, RAF, during the latter's critical illness in the winter of 1944-5 was largely instrumental in saving his life, according to the testimony of Dr. Selwyn-Clark who was a prisoner at this period.*

*Throughout the two years of his imprisonment he displayed qualities of initiative, courage and resource, which in my opinion merit official recognition and reward, whether in the form of promotion to Warrant Officer or commissioned rank, or in whatever other manner considered suitable by superior authority. If further details are required I can supply them at any time.*

It was also in the wake of the Japanese surrender that Colonel Price learned from a Japanese source how the Waichow-Sham Shui Po-Argyle plot had been discovered. One of the loyal Chinese lorry drivers has been caught carrying a message to Colonel Newham at Argyle. Under torture, the driver identified Routledge and Ford and then the others. Having served the Kempeitai's purpose, the Chinese informant had then been executed.

Owing to the extraordinary bravery and unbroken silence of Ford, Newham, Gray, Routledge and Hardy, the senior British and Canadian officers, including General Maltby and his staff in Argyle, and Colonel Price and his Canadian officers such as Major Bishop and Captain LeBoutillier in Sham Shui Po, were never implicated in the smuggling and escape plots, and therefore never penalized. In his post-war report, Colonel Price wrote:

*Distinguished Conduct Medal (DCM)*     *Sergeant Ronald John Routledge, c 194*

*None of us who shared so many experiences with them, can ever forget their bravery and their fortitude under torture of the worst kind. We owe our lives to them.*

After the war, The King awarded all who were arrested or involved in the escape plot the highest military honour that could be bestowed according to their rank.

Sergeant Ronald John Routledge, Royal Canadian Corps of Signals, received the Distinguished Conduct Medal (DCM). He continued to serve in the Canadian Army after the war. With his health recovered, he graduated from Royal Roads Military College, and retired in 1965 with the rank of Captain and the deep gratitude of his country. In October 2010, Canadian Forces Base Kingston dedicated an important new building on the base to remember and to honour the "Quiet Courage" (as his citation reads) of Captain Routledge, DCM. No such honour was more deserved.

Colonel John Price, Royal Rifles of Canada, added to his Military Cross (MC) from World War I the Order of the British Empire (OBE). Colonel (later Brigadier) Price, returned to his senior executive position at Price Brothers, his family-owned forestry company in Quebec. No commanding officer was ever more revered by his men than he.

Captain Douglas Ford, 2nd Battalion, Royal Scots, was posthumously awarded the Distinguished Service Medal (DSM) in 1945. Since I had met Captain Ford in Hong Kong before the battle, and because I was later aware of his heroic reputation, I went to visit the Headquarters of the Royal Scots in Edinburgh Castle with my grandson, Tyler, in 2005. In the centre of the headquarters of this ancient and famous Scottish regiment, is a large picture of Captain Ford, dressed in his kilt, at age 25, just before he was sent to Hong Kong. Beneath is a large plaque which tells his story. It is apparent he is one of the heroes of his regiment, and rightfully so. He certainly is one of mine.

*POW Camp 3D, Yokohama Japan.*

## CHAPTER 6

# The Saboteurs

To compensate for the severe manpower shortage in Japan caused by the war, the Japanese began to ship allied Prisoners of War to Japan to work as slave labourers in coal mines and heavy industrial activity in 1942.

The trip itself was death-defying. Because the Japanese refused to mark their prisoner transport ships with a red cross or some agreed upon symbol to identify them, thousands of allied Prisoners of War were lost at sea when unsuspecting American submarines mistakenly torpedoed some of these transports. One such ship, the *Lisbon Maru*, carrying 1,800 British POWs from Hong Kong to Japan to work as slave labourers, was sunk in the South China sea on October 1, 1942, by the American submarine *USS Grouper*, whose captain had no idea of the precious cargo in the hold of the ship he was attacking. Eight hundred and forty-six prisoners died, either by drowning or shot by the Japanese as they tried to swim clear of the wreck.

Under these dangerous conditions the first draft of 663 Canadian prisoners, of which I was one, left Sham Shui Po under the command of Captain John Reid, a Winnipeg

*The Tatsuta Maru carried 663 Canadian POWs*
*from Hong Kong to Japan on 19 January 1943.*

Grenadiers Medical Officer, on January 19, 1943. Our unmarked transport was the Japanese steamer *Tatsuta Maru*.

After a nightmare trip, made particularly hellish by a dysentery epidemic that broke out in the battened down hold of the ship, we arrived in Japan - dehydrated, starving, half dead, and covered with filth. It turned out we were destined to be put to work in the Nippon Kokan shipbuilding yard in Yokohama, the biggest shipyard in Japan. Employing thousands of Japanese workers, Nippon Kokan built both naval vessels and freighters, ships whose replacement was now the most pressing priority of Japan's war effort due to the severe shipping losses this island nation was suffering from American submarines. Within a day or two of arrival at Prison Camp 3D, just outside of Yokohama, we were sent to the shipyard to begin a work schedule of 13 days on, one day off.

What surprised us all as we were assigned tasks around the shipyard was how little damage it had suffered despite numerous attacks by American heavy bombers. The rising rate of production of urgently needed ships seemed to be unaffected by the attacks. C.A. "Charlie" Clark, a fellow prisoner at Camp 3D, was particularly struck by this lack of success of the allied bombing campaign, and that got him thinking.

Clark was an unusual individual who, besides his current service in "C-Force", had served as a Canadian soldier in World War I and been wounded at Vimy Ridge in 1917. Born in England, Clark emigrated to Canada and enlisted in the Canadian army in 1915. He had spent most of his civilian career as an employee in Canada's Postal Service and in 1940 volunteered again, now age 44, to serve in Canada's army. Because of his postal experience and previous army record Clark was quickly promoted to the rank of Staff Sergeant and placed in charge of the "C-Force" Postal Service at Brigade Headquarters. During the battle of Hong Kong he distinguished himself for his courage and devotion to duty.

Clark realized that the Nippon Kokan shipyard was a critical factor in Japanese war production, essential to Japan's survival. He knew that a successful attack on the shipyard – he was already thinking of an "inside job" - would hit the Japanese where it would hurt the most. He also knew the consequences for anyone caught committing even the smallest hostile act against Nippon Kokan. Secrecy was paramount, but as he began to plot his sabotage Clark realized he would need at least one accomplice. After careful consideration he approached Private Stanley Cameron of the Royal Canadian Ordnance Corps. He had chosen well. Cameron immediately volunteered to risk his life with Clark and never to reveal anything about the plot that they now set out to concoct. The first step was to assess the target.

A Japanese shipyard is a complicated industrial creation, a steel fabrication process employing every kind of skill, from metal workers to acetylene welders. In 1943, the basic process to build a seagoing vessel was as follows:
• A marine engineer designed and committed to paper, in blue print form, drawings of every single part, from the tiniest to the largest, that makes up a complete ship.

• The images, design, shape and dimension of each part of the ship were then rendered into moulds - wooden templates that were life-size versions of the parts described in the blueprints.

• The templates were then used to trace the shape of each part on steel plate so that acetylene torches could cut the steel to the precise outline of the form. As each part was cut from steel sheets, it was transferred to the appropriate vessel under construction and riveted, welded or bolted into the ship.

*Yokohama, January 28, 1945. Nippon Kokan Shipyard.*

If one was intent on sabotaging the shipyard, what on the huge site was the best target? Where was the point of greatest vulnerability? Where and how could two prisoners possibly cause significant damage in such an enormous, spread out, decentralized industrial enterprise covering many square miles of heavy machinery and equipment and thousands of watchful Japanese workers?

By going for the soft spot. The point of vulnerability that Clark identified was the Japanese practice of storing all the ships' blueprints and all the wooden moulds in two

*Nippon Kokan Shipyard, Yokohama, 2014.*

buildings adjacent to one another. Destroy those buildings, Clark reasoned, along with the blueprints and wooden forms in them - those designs and prototypes essential to the creation of every part of every vessel in the yard – and work in the shipyard would come to a standstill.

The crucial question, of course, was how? Since the yard only worked on a day shift, whatever preparations made for sabotage would have to be executed in broad daylight, right under the noses of the watchful Japanese, while the destructive operation itself would have to take place at night when only a few watchmen were on guard.

The sabotage Clark decided on was arson, timed to occur after dark. The method would be a cleverly contrived "time bomb." From their work sites Clark and Cameron began filching and squirreling away a medley of combustibles such as paint, paint thinner, oil, oil soaked rags, oil soaked shavings, benzine, resin, paper, chemicals and celluloid – a flammable combination guaranteed to cause an instant inferno when lit. The fuse would be a candle, timed to burn down for several hours before igniting the incendiary materials.

It took Clark and Cameron a year, acting in secret even from their fellow POWs, to gain regular access to the target buildings, to establish a safe hiding place for the "bomb," then to smuggle in the combustibles and put the device together, all the while knowing that an unexpected search or a single mistake would lead to a most certain and horrible death.

It is one thing in the heat of battle to act courageously and instinctively to save yourself or your comrades. This kind of courage was of a higher degree. To coolly plot and prepare for such a daring act of sabotage, knowing full well the risk and the consequences, takes something beyond the bounds of courage. It took two remarkable Canadian soldiers who were willing to continue the fight to the very centre of their enemy's heartland.

On January 18, 1944, Clark and Cameron were finally ready. Shortly before quitting time they set up the device behind some rubbish in one of the little used and rarely inspected store rooms in the mould loft, lit the makeshift candle fuse, then marched back to Camp 3D with their comrades. At eight that night, with Clark and Cameron and their fellow POWs safely in camp and accounted for, the candle burned down to the ignition point (celluloid shavings accumulated from soap boxes), the shavings and other combustibles burst into flames and soon the storage building and then neighbouring buildings were engulfed in a raging inferno.

The result was everything Clark and Cameron had hoped for. In one night the massive shipyard ground to a flaming, then smoldering halt. While in the days to come some limited work recommenced on a few nearly-finished ships, all new ship construction ceased, including work on the Japanese anti-submarine naval vessels so desperately needed by the Japanese Navy for the war at sea. They'd done it. Two brave Canadian prisoners of war had accomplished what the American Air Force had so far been unable to: put Nippon Kokan largely out of action.

To say that the Japanese were furious and appalled at this catastrophe is an understatement, and the Kempeitai were soon in our camp questioning the Canadian Warrant Officers and anyone else they suspected. Two things blocked their discovery of the truth. First, the secrecy had been total between Clark and Cameron. No one else knew anything to tell. We POWs were as in the dark as the enraged Japanese. Secondly, Clark and Cameron left no telltale signs in the ashes of the fire or the surroundings that could be traced to the POW workers at the shipyard.

Ironically, it soon became clear amid the uproar that our Japanese Camp Commandant was himself not anxious to find out that the POWs under his command were guilty of arson, a finding that most certainly would have led to his court martial and a sentence of death. Better to conclude, officially, that spontaneous combustion was the culprit. In these curious circumstances the investigation ground on, with Clark and Cameron watching with trepidation for any sign that their plot had been exposed. But no evidence was discovered, and finally the heat of the investigation began to die down.

The final irony is that our claims of innocence were probably accepted thanks to the arrogant Japanese conclusion that we Canadian POWs would have neither the skill nor the courage to do such a thing.

*Epilogue*

Nippon Kokan was seriously crippled. With little or no manual work to be done at the shipyard, the prisoners of Camp 3D were divided up and transferred north to work in mining camps in Ohasi and Sendai where we were until the end of the war. Without regret, but with a chuckle or two, we left the hated shipyard and the puzzled Japanese police behind.

Lieutenant-Commander Edward V. Dockweiler, USN, who was the senior Allied Officer at Camp 3D at the time of our departure, wrote a report on the Nippon Kokan fire for the American and Canadian military authorities after his release from prison camp in 1945. The key points of his report are as follows:

*About 20:00 hours on 18 January 1944, a large fire broke out in this yard, completely destroying the steel shed, ships outfitting stores, prisoner of war mess hall, riggers lobby, tool rooms, part of the shipfitters shop and mould loft.*

*At this time, the yard was engaged in building escort destroyers and merchant shipping.*

*Its tonnage production was about 8,000 tons per month.*

*The fire was started by Staff Sergeant Clark, Canadian Postal Corps. and Private K.S. Cameron, Royal Canadian ordnance Corps....*

*This act of sabotage greatly crippled the production of this yard and directly minimized the Japanese war effort, and the contribution to the Allied War effort that these two men made under the handicap of being prisoners of war, cannot be overestimated. Their conduct as prisoners of war, while under my jurisdiction, was exemplary and fulfilled the highest traditions of the Canadian Army.*

Staff Sergeant Clark and Private Cameron escaped detection and both survived to return home to their families after the war. For their brave actions they were decorated by the King. "Charlie" Clark won the Distinguished Conduct Medal (DCM) and Private Cameron the Military Medal (MM).

Clark became an energetic leader of the returning Canadians soldiers and eventually formed the Hong Kong Veterans Association of Canada. Ironically, this brave man died in a house fire, and with him perished his unpublished account and his notes of how he and Cameron had so bravely carried the war to their enemy.

*The Distinguished Conduct Medal (DCM).*　　*Staff Sergeant Charles Albert Clark, September 1945.*

After recovering his health, Private Cameron became a very valuable member of his local community. He was a "Big Brother" and a member of both the Kiwanis Club and The Canadian Institute for the Blind (CNIB), where he taught the blind to play golf and to curl. It is a measure of the modesty of this brave man that his daughter could say of him: "Until Dad died I never knew he was awarded any military medals or that he was a war hero." He would probably say in his quiet way, "I was just doing my duty."

*The Military Medal (MM).*　　　　*Corporal Kenneth Stanley Cameron September 1941.*

*Doctor John Reid, September 1941.*

CHAPTER 7
# The Doctor

This is a story of another kind of courage, the story of the determination and character of a man who, despite the risks, never gave up in his unending struggle to save the lives of those under his command, both as their doctor and their commanding officer. Instead of his own well being and safety, he focussed not on himself, but solely on the well being of his men. This is the story of Major John Anthony Gibson Reid MBE.

For most of my time as a POW, I served as a warrant officer under the direct command of Captain Reid in Camp 3D-Yokohama.

John Reid graduated in 1938 from the University of Toronto Medical School, the year before the war began. After his residency, he joined the Royal Canadian Army Medical Corps as a Captain. In the fall of 1941, he was sent to Hong Kong with "C-Force" as a medical officer.

He was in the thick of the battle of Hong Kong working as a doctor on the battlefield, or just behind the lines in makeshift hospitals, to save the lives of the wounded. He proved to be a powerhouse in his role as a doctor, where he saved the lives of many badly wounded Canadian soldiers.

After his capture, Captain Reid utilized all his ingenuity and skill to minister to the Prisoners of War in Hong Kong both in North Point and in Sham Shui Po Camp. His patients, forced into slave labour and starvation, suffered from every form of illness, from beriberi to diphtheria. These diseases were caused or worsened by the lack of even minimal nutrition and terrible living conditions.

With little or no medicine or medical equipment, nor help from the Japanese, Reid laboured non-stop to save as many of his patients in the prison camp as he could.

In the medical diary he kept secret from the Japanese through the war, Reid presents a composite of the average physical state of the Canadian prisoners of war at Sham Shui Po Camp by the end of 1942, a year since the surrender at Hong Kong.
Reid writes:

*"Rifleman X is not so well as some of his fellows, but much better than others. He can and does go on work parties, at least part of the time. He is very thin, having lost 20 per cent (on average, 36 lb.) of his former body weight, and he appears about 50 years old, though his real age is 30....There are cracks at the corner of the mouth and patches of dermatitis in and around the nose. He has a deep ulcer on the calf of the left leg. His tongue is sore, smooth and red, with a deep furrow down the centre. Two teeth are chipped from biting on pebbles in his rice, and several other teeth are grossly carious so that he has difficulty in chewing his food.....He complains he cannot read ordinary print, but he can make out newspaper headlines. Bright sunlight causes excessive lacrimation....He complains of constriction, like a band, around his chest....His history includes malaria with two relapses [and] he has just recovered from one of several attacks of diarrhea. He states that both lower extremities are numb from thigh level to the toes....The right great toe is deformed where a tropical*

*ulcer has healed....He staggers in the dark, but manages moderately well in the daytime....He has some numbness of the hands, especially the finger tips...Nocturnal frequency of urination...has disturbed his sleep for so long that he regards it an as integral part of his existence....He...does not appear greatly concerned over the usual anxieties of life."*

As Mentioned earlier, when we arrived in Japan, we were sent to Camp 3D in Yokohama to work in the nearby Nippon Kokan Shipyard. The Japanese Camp Commander of Camp 3D was Lieutenant Uwamori.

When Reid arrived at Camp 3D the camp was empty and he found a shoddy collection of adjoining bunkhouses made of 1/4 inch plywood. The buildings had no heating arrangements, dirt floors, and the men were expected to sleep on two tier platforms on coconut fiber mats. Against the cold, the prisoners were issued with useless porous blankets made from wood fiber. There was no hospital, no dispensary, no medical equipment, no medical supplies and an untrained Japanese medical orderly who tried to assume command of all medical operations.

The Japanese demanded a work quota, to be filled from the camp each day, with no regard to who was well enough to make it to the shipyard, let alone fit to work. The result was chaos and occasionally a dying man was forced to go to work, while men better able to work were excused.

The predicament Reid found himself in was daunting. The Japanese intent was to extract the most work from the most men on the least amount of food possible. Work quotas were demanded daily and men already debilitated by 13 months of captivity and labour in Hong Kong were now forced to work 12 hours a day, 13 days out of 14 at all sorts of drudgery from hull painting on high, shaky scaffolding to lugging cement, welding (without protective goggles), scraping rust off steel plates and tarring everything from ropes to railway undercarriages. Many sick prisoners were sent out to work, barely able to drag themselves to the shipyard. Those who were slow or complained of illness on the job were beaten by brutal guards who were deaf and blind to the men's obvious weakness and physical impairment.

Aside from the few medicines and some ration supplements that Reid had brought with him from Hong Kong - supplies that were soon exhausted - the only relief he could prescribe for the sick was rest, in other words, exemption from work. Jousting with the Japanese authorities about who was too sick to work, the need for more food, medicines, bandages, boots and warmer clothes was a deadly struggle for Reid that began on our arrival at 3D and never ended. From the outset his daily stock in trade was a program of personal persuasiveness, logical argument, tough negotiation and unending stress.

On this issue, in dangerous personal clashes more than once, he stood between a sick prisoner and a Japanese guard, rather than allow the prisoner to be forced to work or to be further abused.

Somehow, Major Reid took command of this situation, and despite some dangerous confrontations with the various levels of Japanese authority which could have led to charges of insubordination and execution, he gained the sole right to decide who could go to work and who would not. This victory was crucial to preserve the lives of many of the prisoners in these conditions.

However, something else began to happen. Reid was able to alter the behaviour and mood of the camp administration. Based on his personal determination and his charisma alone, he persuaded the Japanese to be less demanding and more sympathetic to their prisoners. He argued, better treatment would lead to better work at the shipyard. His main target for change was the aloof Camp

Commander, Captain Uwamori.

Gradually, Reid persuaded Uwamori that permitting violent beatings, often handed out in the camp by his subordinates on a whim, must be stopped. Reid persuaded Uwamori that such savage behaviour was uncivilized by international standards, and was dishonourable conduct for a Japanese officer. This could easily have backfired.

Eventually, Uwamori agreed that his subordinates could not abuse prisoners without his prior personal approval. This, in effect, put a stop to the serious physical violence in Camp 3D.

Of course, once Reid persuaded him to this course, it dawned on Uwamori that he, and he alone, would henceforth bear the burden and the full responsibility in Reid's eyes for any future abuse of prisoners. This was a vital breakthrough as these beatings could hasten the death of a desperately malnourished and fragile prisoner whose recovery resources were often nil. This course of action was fraught with danger for Reid and at any moment could have led to his own death for offending the touchy medieval Japanese sense of honour or, as mentioned earlier, to a charge of insubordination against the Japanese POW code, which made insubordination of any kind punishable by death.

Now the climate in the camp improved as the Canadian Medical Officer's powerful persuasive will began to replace the former violence, chaos and humiliation directed at prisoners by their captors as in the past.

Next, Reid persuaded Uwamori that he, as a Japanese officer, should share with Reid in the humanitarian task of saving POW lives as a matter of compassion, humanity and decency, and above all as an honourable thing to do. Hesitant at first, Uwamori began, despite the awful risks to him as a Camp Commandant, to buy and smuggle into Reid's hands certain vitally needed drugs, serums and medical supplies from the black market.

Uwamori, while trying to avoid the charge of "traitor" from his Japanese subordinates, began little by little to improve life and conditions in the camp. He approved wood burning camp stoves for the winter. He ordered hot baths with soap for the prisoners once a month, as well as a "steam machine" to delouse prisoner's clothes.

These changes improved upon the conditions of the past. The sick responded favourably to the drugs and medicine now becoming available to Reid.

While Captain Reid had no formal training as a military officer, he was perhaps the best leader and most respected officer I ever saw. He had a remarkable way with men, either his own or the Japanese.

This young Canadian officer now became the conscience and the very moral soul of this camp.

I was struck early on in Japan by Reid's ability, with only three months training and no line officer training, to assume command and win the respect not only of the men under his care, but soon after our arrival at Camp 3D, that of the Japanese.

He had the calming, commanding personality of a natural leader, but his authority on both sides of the wire was based on his strength of character: absolute honesty; absolute fairness in dealing with us in his unrelenting efforts to protect us, medically and otherwise; a toughness that under years of pressure never cracked; and the courage to stand up to the Japanese until Reid was close to God to both his own men, and the Japanese.

A crucial contribution of Reid to his men was hope. He always made it clear that he knew we would win this war, that it was just a matter of time, we would succeed, no question about it. He never, never for a moment, left any doubt. He knew that if the sicker soldiers thought we were going to lose this war, they would have died in 24 hours.

*The Japanese Prison Staff of Camp 3D Yokohama. Lt. Uwamori centre front row.*

They would have thought: "Why try to stay alive, why put up with this if we're going to lose anyway?" Captain Reid said, "Put up with it. We aren't going to lose. It's just a matter of time. These people will never defeat us.We can see it through!"

His inspirational, positive "Yes we can" attitude and his optimism buoyed up even the most depressed. He was as fair as he was reasonable. He would listen, but no one ever had any doubt that he was in charge. And no one ever doubted that he should be the boss. No soldier ever questioned his decision as to who would work and who was excused from the work party. Respect for him was universal and no one would even dream of disputing his orders or, worse still, of disappointing him.

Reid knew full well, as did Uwamori, the risk they were running, that some of Uwamori's senior military staff might accuse him of being soft on prisoners, and Reid of insubordination to the immutable Japanese Prisoner Code. Nonetheless, they carried on to make camp 3D as bearable as possible. Reid's leadership saved many Canadian lives, but never at the cost of being obsequious. This led to the respect of the Japanese.

A constant nagging issue for the men through their time in prison camp was the division of rations. The variable was that each day's quantity of rice and soup was affected by the number of sick who were off work: those who couldn't work were assigned one-half, sometimes one-third rations, a practice Reid pointed out to the Japanese would hinder their recovery and therefore their ability to work. But stuck with the rule, the mess system Reid set up as the most fair and reassuring to the men, a system he supervised himself to ensure compliance, was that all food was pooled at every meal and each man, whether working or off sick, received the same amount.

This was a stand Reid maintained consistently against

direct Japanese orders to put sick men who weren't working on reduced rations. Reid saw the Japanese disregard for individual life, the readiness, in this case to consign the sick to the rubbish heap, simply as part of their culture at the time, an understanding he took into account in his dealings with them. He would argue with the Japanese how foolish it was. At great risk of a charge of insubordination he would then say, "You have given us the order and if we disobey, please don't look too closely." To let them save face, he promised to feed the sick men the reduced ration, and of course didn't do so. We were going to get through this together.

Since to starving men the fairness of food distribution is of such vital importance, Reid's decision to control it on a personal basis demonstrated his awareness that he could never delegate this responsibility to anyone else.Because of Reid, there was little of the tension and rebellion over food distribution experienced in other POW camps.

A strategy that Reid evolved to increase the food supply was to sell the Japanese on granting more rations to prisoners doing less work than normal, but enough to warrant more food than if they were off sick completely. He instituted "slow walking groups" made up of prisoners who would march to Nippon Kokan at their own slower pace and, once there, do sit-down jobs like sorting and cleaning nuts and bolts. Variations of this were prisoners who went to work every other day, or every three days, resting up in between. In camp, Reid convened what he called the "anvil chorus," beriberi patients who sat outside on good days and straightened welding rods with hammers – hammering away for ten minutes, then resting for five. All of this limited activity brought in more food without doing harm to the sick men involved.

Soon after the Canadian sabotage, which virtually shut down the shipyard in January of 1944 (described in Chapter

6), the Japanese began shipping surplus POW labour to Northern prison camps such as Sendai and Ohasi.

On May 12, 1945, Camp 3D was closed and Captain Reid and 200 prisoners were sent to North Sendai Camp #1, and I and 200 others were sent to the mining camp at Ohasi.

Sendai Camp #1, the Joban Coal Mine prison camp, was located in the mountains on the east coast of Japan. It had been in operation since April 1943 and held a mix of prisoners – 135 Dutch and 232 British – who toiled in terrible conditions a thousand meters below the surface. There, at the coal face, two kilometers into the mountains from the mine entrance, the temperature hovered at 50' C, the air was stale, toxic and thick with coal dust, and the men sloshed through water up to their knees, sometimes their bellies.

There were three shifts, with men at work in the mine 24 hours a day. One shift started at three in the morning and came back at one in the afternoon, another started at noon and came back about 10 at night, and the third started at eight at night and came back at six in the morning.

For light, the men wore caps holding miners' lamps powered by wet cell batteries attached to the rubber belts at their waists, which was one cause of mine injuries. Because of the heat, the men wore nothing but loin cloths down "the hole." The batteries could detach from their flimsy belts when they were working and burn their backs and buttocks. Regularly, men would collapse at the coal face for lack of oxygen.

Above ground, the living conditions were comparably awful. The huts were the filthiest Reid had ever seen - old, rickety, with papery walls mostly torn away and dirt-stiff sleeping mats infested with vermin. This was the work place and sleep environment the Canadians were now thrown into.

Since the camp's opening, the treatment of the Dutch and British prisoners by the Japanese camp staff had been barbarous, and the morale of these prisoners was, by now, at rock bottom.

Reid's diary continues:

*The conditions down in the mine were very bad in another way. The Japanese who worked down there were the lowest type I ran into. Little above animals. These were "Sensei," or professors — supposed in Japanese culture to be the bosses and teachers of men. Very many were extremely brutal and cruel, and when they themselves got down under these atrocious conditions they seemed to almost go insane....It was a regular thing for the men to be very badly beaten....To give an example of what happened down there, one of these Sensei started to beat one of our men...the Sensei kicked and beat him and got him down on the floor and then fell on him and bit him in the thigh.*

As at 3D, Reid began his relentless protests to the Commandant: Again from his diary:

*When we began to work in this situation, the Canadian group particularly, we rapidly got this stuff cut down and, finally, almost completely cut out. We complained to the Commandant about every single case of a beating, with all the details. He [Commandant Chezwa] was a better type and got the company officials in, and got the Sensei in, and warned them again and again....After the first six weeks there were no beatings in the Canadian group. They still beat the Dutch and English. They'd been in the camp so long they'd given up hope.*

Reid had left one hell-hole of a camp for another, where he continued to work tirelessly as a doctor to save as many men as he could. I later heard that as he sensed that the war was coming to an end, he fought even harder to bring as many of his men home safely as he could.

After the war, Uwamori was charged by the War Crimes Tribunal of the Far East with a serious offense against Canadian POWs. If he had been found guilty, he would have been sentenced to death.

When Reid heard of this, he entered a plea in Uwamori's defense, and with skill and conviction convinced the court that Uwamori's conversion deserved clemency. As a result, instead of the death sentence for Uwamori, the court sentenced him to a prison term which, after a short while, was commuted to a suspended sentence.

In a letter of thanks written to Reid in Canada a year later, Uwamori described the story of his arrest and trial, and of his release and homecoming:

*How I can express the greatest joy I ever felt in my life. Arrived home in the evening of the big day. I was welcomed by my family and we could not stop hugging each other and shedding tears. I think I could imagine your deep emotion which you might have felt when you came home after the war.*

*It was entirely of your favour to enable me to get rid of such a very hard case. I hereby explain (sic) my sincerest gratitude for your fairness and kindness shown to me during and after the war.*

Uwamori, 1989.

*If you allow me, I wish to write you often and see you anytime after normal relationship is revived between your country and Japan. Never would I forget your efforts, kindness and fairness as long as I live.*

Japan was devastated in the years after the war. Uwamori, like most Japanese, struggled during that period of national reconstruction to rebuild his life. A year after Uwamori's letter, a long, battered parcel arrived on Reid's doorstep in Toronto marked "Bunch of Canes" – evidently the only gift that Masao Uwamori, under the straightened circumstances of that time in Japan, could cobble together as an offering of thanks.

Reid's act of chivalry to his former enemy during this black period of hatred for the Japanese and the allied desire for revenge, came as a dramatic sign to the people of Japan that perhaps, led by the example of men like Captain Reid, a better future lay ahead. This act of decency, forgiveness and fair play, instead of showing hatred and revenge to this enemy officer, was just one of the commendable qualities of this great man. It was prompted by a bond that had been forged in war. When Reid needed Uwamori in his deadly game to save our lives as well as his own, Uwamori helped. When Uwamori needed Reid, to see justice done, Reid helped Uwamori. On his death bed, many years later, among Uwamori's last words was a statement of his gratitude and his deep respect for Reid once again.

The Official History of the Canadian Medical Services 1939-1945 echoes this praise:

*The measure of his success in extracting every possible concession from the Japanese, and in making the fullest use of the most inadequate medical facilities, and in persuading his fellow prisoners to make the best of things, is that only 23 of this particular group died. This, the largest group of Canadians in Japan, had the smallest number of deaths.*

The outcome speaks volumes for this outstanding officer and doctor. Captain Reid's medical skill was exceptional, and aided by his sense of duty, his determination, and his courage, it is estimated that his singular effort reduced the death rate of the prisoners under his command to less than a quarter of what it was in other camps in Japan.

He survived the war and, with great honour, returned home to his family. Soon after his return, to advance his knowledge, he took up a fellowship in cardiology at the Toronto General and Wellesley Hospitals.

In *Long Night's Journey into Day*, a major post-war medical study by Dr. Charles G. Roland concerning the medical problems of treating Japanese POWs, Reid receives major credit and fulsome praise for his lifesaving work in Japan. In the long history of our Canadian Medical Officers in World War I and in World War II, no one surpassed the skill, ingenuity and leadership of Major John Anthony Gibson Reid.

For his exceptional bravery and his meritorious service far beyond the call of duty, the King promoted him to Major, and awarded the coveted MBE (Member of the Most Excellent Order of the British Empire). He was later inducted into the "Canadian Veteran's Hall of Valour," by his fellow veterans.

How Reid, day after day, week after week, month

*Member of the Most Excellent Order of the British Empire medal awarded to Major John Anthony Gibson Reid MBE.*

after month and year after year for nearly four years, stood the stress of his role in these hell-hole camps is almost incomprehensible. He was all alone, his only powers were persuasion and his iron will to ignore the personal risks and to persevere. Why he didn't crack under this continuous stress is a tribute to his character, his physical and mental strength, his sense of duty, and his courage. He should have been awarded the Victoria Cross, but he would have laughed at that. He knew that deep in the hearts and minds of his soldiers, his fellow officers, and even his enemies, he had won the only honour that really means anything. He also knew that he had done his duty - and then some - and to him that's all that mattered.

*Doctor John Reid, post war.*

After Captain, now Major, Reid returned home, he soon began to suffer from ill health. It was ironic that for his efforts, his reward was a crippling disease directly related to his service which led to an early death.

I last saw him at Camp 3D Yokohama on the day I was being transferred north to the Ohasi camp. He shook my hand and, as he returned my last salute, he gave me his big positive smile and said, "Goodbye George," and wished me, "Good luck."

If the true measure of a man is how, at great personal risk, he braves, defies, and overcomes even the worst conditions imaginable, then he met that test in full measure.

I never saw him again, but with me and "his boys" the memory of this great man will live forever.

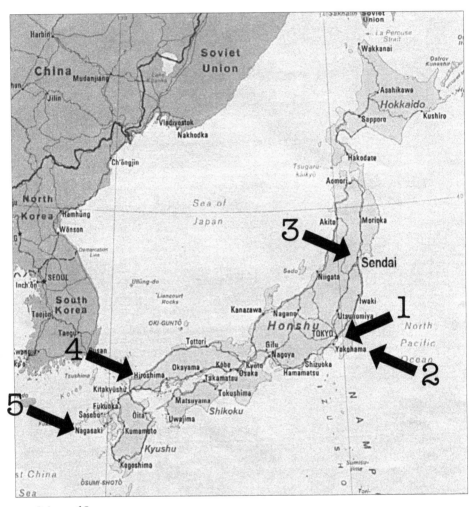

Map of Japan

1. Tokyo

2. Prison Camp 3D, Yokohama

3. Prison Camp, Ohasi

4. Site of first Atomic Bomb, Hiroshima, August 6, 1945

5. Site of second Atomic Bomb, Nagasaki, August 9, 1945

CHAPTER 8

# The Secret Radio

This story revolves around an American sailor named Jerry Bunch, but it also involves his Canadian comrades, we who shared the last six months of imprisonment with him in the Japanese POW camp at Ohasi and who benefited from his bravery after our transfer there in the winter of 1945. For at the risk of his life, Jerry Bunch, USN, was the wizard who built a radio at Ohasi and established contact with the outside world, and by doing so slayed for his camp mates the greatest demon of demoralization, total isolation, when the daily life of a prisoner of war is so devoid of news or hope that it sometimes seems as though the world outside the prison camp has ceased to exist.

The story begins in November 1942 when the Japanese sent a group of allied prisoners, mostly Americans, to a remote camp at Ohasi in the mountains of northern Japan. Here they were forced to mine iron ore in intolerable conditions, deep underground.

The prisoners were completely isolated from the outside world at Ohasi. The Japanese labourers who worked in the mine alongside them were illiterate peasants who were

*Ohasi Prison Camp, Sendai Japan, 1945.*

terrified of the guards and at the same time blindly devoted to the Emperor, believing absolutely in Japan's final victory and the triumphant outcome of Japan's aggression in South East Asia. Anything these peasants had to say was unreliable. On the other hand, information intentionally communicated to the POWs by the Japanese authorities was all bluff and nonsense, to the point of absurdity. From their chronic boasting one would have thought that the entire United States Navy was being sunk every three months, then rebuilt from scratch so that Japan could sink it again!

As the incarceration at Ohasi dragged on for these men, the lack of war news, the uncertainty of rescue, the uncertainty of relief from starvation, and the terrible, unending toil in the mines all conspired to lower morale and have very serious negative effects on the physical and mental health of the prisoners. Deprived of even a shred of reliable news from the outside world, many of them began to feel they had been abandoned and forgotten and that the Japanese were right: there was no hope for them.

Enter Jerry Bunch, Radioman 1st Class. Jerry was serving on the American heavy cruiser *USS Houston*, as a radio technician when she was sunk in the battle of the Sunda Strait off the coast of Java in March 1942. After the sinking, Jerry and his shipmates survived in shark-infested waters for 11 hours before reaching land. Of a crew of 1,080, 759 *Houston* sailors lost their lives. Jerry and his fellow survivors were subsequently captured by the Japanese and became prisoners of war. Jerry was imprisoned first in Java, then at Changi prison in Singapore, before being transferred to the Ohasi mining camp in Northern Japan in November 1942. As a skilled electronics technician, Jerry was assigned to work in the mine's electrical repair shop, above ground.

Jerry did not come to Ohasi empty-handed. When he and his comrades were taken prisoner in Java, then a Dutch colony, they were billeted at first in civilian buildings commandeered by the Japanese as temporary POW quarters. Oversight was somewhat lax at first, and the quarters had not been thoroughly inspected by the Japanese. It was in these circumstances that Jerry Bunch and two other survivors from the *Houston*, Machinist 1st Class Jack Feliz and Army Sergeant Jesse Stanbrough, discovered a Philco radio that had been left behind by its Dutch owner. For the rest of the time they were held in Java, under Jerry's direction, he and his mates operated this

*Philco Model 40-120C Table Radio.*

secret radio in the camp and kept pace with war news. When the three friends were moved to Singapore, they cannibalized the Philco radio, and smuggled as many of the components out of the Java camp as they could safely conceal, in hopes of reconstructing a radio at a future destination. But vital parts had to be left behind, and no possibility of acquiring replacements appeared until some time after their arrival at Ohasi. The break came when the mine officials began to allow the local villagers to bring their civilian radios to the mine's electrical shop to be serviced and repaired. This work was often assigned to Jerry, one of the most skilled technicians, and it was now, unknown to any of his fellow prisoners except Feliz and Stanbrough and risking a brutal death at the hands of Kempeitai if he was found out, that Jerry Bunch set in motion a plan to build a secret two-way radio that would allow the camp to learn news of the war's progress and, just possibly, to make contact with the allies when possible rescue was imminent.

The genius of the plan was Jerry, and his almost magical ability to repair the villagers' radios and somehow make them work again despite some electronic thievery – his removal now of a resister, now of a condenser, now of a vacuum tube from the sets he was working on, to be saved and used in the construction of his own secret radio. In servicing civilian radios, Jerry now had a source for parts. The trick was to establish a safe conduit for getting the components from the mine's electrical shop back to camp, where the radio would eventually be put together.

His simple solution (its simplicity another mark of genius) was a big floppy hat, acquired in a trade with one of his comrades, combined with Jerry's strategy of exercising extreme patience. From then on, like some sort of hat fetishist, he began to wear his new headgear day and night, indoors and out, awake or asleep. Like everyone returning to camp after the day's work, he was subjected to a careful

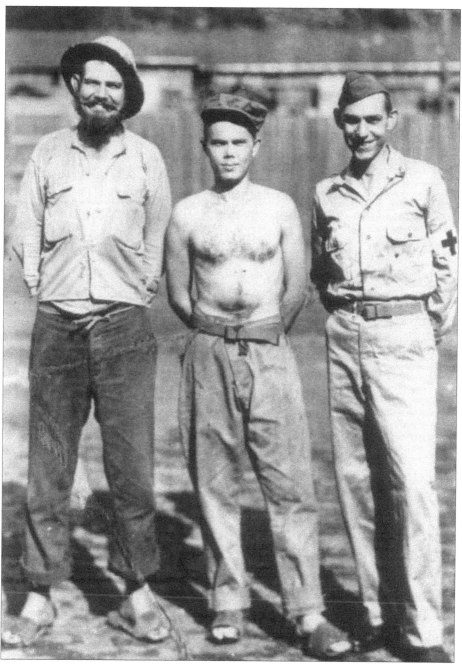

*Jack Feliz, Jerry Judson Bunch (wearing floppy hat), Lt. Tucker, Ohasi Prison Camp, September 15, 1945.*

search by the guards, and from the day he first sported his new hat and for many days afterwards the guards in patting him down would carefully check the hat for contraband. But as the days and weeks went by, the guards, never finding a thing, occasionally began to ignore the ridiculous, ubiquitous hat until, finally, they stopped checking it altogether. Feeling as safe as he ever would, Jerry Bunch skillfully altered the hat by creating a false bottom inside, with a hidden compartment between the false bottom and the crown. Now, piece by piece, the precious radio parts began sailing into camp stashed in the secret compartment of Jerry's big floppy hat.

In executing his careful, patient, yet highly dangerous plan, Jerry was helped by his comrades Feliz and Stanbrough. Stanbrough worked in the electrical shop with Jerry. Feliz stole a carbide lantern from the mine, a reflector and a carbide jet, which was broken down and smuggled into the camp, piece by piece, by Jerry. The lantern was used to heat a soldering iron, also stolen, which was essential for the construction of the radio. Construction of the radio was a tense, time-tricky affair because the only private place the work could be done out of sight was in the latrine.

In the summer of 1944, after months of clandestine effort, the radio was finally complete and operational. It was hidden between the outer and inner walls of the camp building and could only be accessed by a removable panel just above Jerry Bunch's upper bunk, a hiding place that narrowly escaped discovery on several occasions when the Kempeitai made surprise searches of the barracks. One night, discovery of a different sort was narrowly missed. Testing the transmission capability of his radio, Jerry suddenly picked up a response to his signal from a U.S. destroyer: "Read you loud and clear," signaled the destroyer's radioman, "where are you?" On hearing "POW Camp, Ohasi," the radioman replied in an instant: "For

God's sake, shut down!" He knew, and now so did Jerry, that radio signals were being monitored by the Japanese, and could be traced. As luck would have it, not this time.

When we Canadian prisoners of war arrived at Ohasi in February 1945, Jerry's secret radio had been in operation for more than six months. Every night before lights out he would take advantage of the hubbub of men chatting and preparing for bed to mask the squealing of the radio as he tuned into the two stations his receiver could pick up: BBC's worldwide service and station KGO in San Francisco. Later in the night, the radio tuned while the camp was sleeping, Jerry would listen to the details of the war's progress, the heartening information of victory on many fronts that would be quietly disseminated throughout the camp. After years of living in a vacuum, this lifeline to the outside world and the news that victory was nigh had a hugely beneficial effect on the outlook and mental health of Jerry's camp mates. An end to the suffering was in sight.

We Canadians arrived at Ohasi from Camp 3D in Yokohama more aware of the war's progress than the Americans had been before Jerry's secret radio. We had worked with the Japanese in the shipyard. The huge American bombing raids we had witnessed from camp, including the fire bombing of Tokyo, and the devastation we saw as we traveled north by train to Ohasi, were dramatic evidence of the tide turning in the allies' favour, of the Japanese lack of means, and of their vulnerability to attack. We knew the allies were going to win the war. The big question for us was, would we survive until the end?

Naturally, we were subjected to the same Japanese arrogance and flights of fancy as the Americans had been, even though the war was now running badly against the Japanese. They repeatedly insisted that after Japan conquered Canada, as, they boasted, it was sure to do, we would never be allowed to go home to our families. The

Japanese reveled in trying to humiliate us, in assuring us that there was no hope in this life for any of us. Trying to demoralize us, as well as working us to death in the mine, were evidently very satisfying experiences to the Japanese psyche, and perhaps a way of bolstering their own well-deserved sense of inferiority. It was also a sign of their instability and unpredictability: what would they do when defeat inevitably came?

This is where the two-way capability of Jerry's secret radio came into play for us all. We knew that 1st Lieutenant Yoshida Zenkichi, our Japanese camp commander and a man who spoke good English, had specific written orders to put us to death, with absolutely no exceptions, in the event that our rescue might be effected by the landing of an allied rescue force. It is well documented that this order to kill prisoners who might be rescued, were actually carried

*Japanese Camp Commandant Lieut Zenkichi (centre)*
*with Ohasi Japanese prison staff, c 1944.*

*Atomic Bomb, Hiroshima,*          *Atomic Bomb, Nagasaki,*
*August 6, 1945.*                  *August 9, 1945.*

out by Japanese execution squads in Tarawa, Mauru, Ballale and Wake Island. Without Jerry's radio we would have no way of knowing if a rescue force had landed and was close at hand, and no way of receiving instructions from them or of coordinating internal action such as a mass uprising in the camp to help our rescuers at the critical moment. In the end, the radio played just such a role.

On August 7, 1945, Jerry Bunch heard a broadcast announcing the American bombing of Hiroshima the day before, a bombing that had used a new weapon of massive, unheard of destructive power. This startling news was disseminated very carefully to a select few among the prisoners. We watched the Japanese carefully to see if they, too, had learned of the bombing. Would this terrifying new allied capability cause Emperor Hirohito to surrender, we wondered? And if he did, how would our captors react? But Lieutenant Zenkichi and the guards showed no signs of disturbance and there was no change in routine. We, we

*Japanese listen to Emperor Hirohito's surrender broadcast, August 15 1945.*

realized, had heard this momentous news before our captors!

Three days later, Jerry Bunch reported to a select few the destruction of Nagasaki, once again by use of an atomic bomb. How, we speculated, could Japan possibly continue to hold out in the face of such destructive might? By now our captors were also aware of these enormous developments and we knew we had entered that foreseen and most dangerous time period when Japanese defeat was a certainty but our immediate personal safety and our rescue by allies were anything but.

This tense time came to a head on August 15, when Emperor Hirohito broadcast to his people the news that Japan was surrendering to the allies. The war, reported Jerry Bunch, was over!

But at Ohasi a dangerous confrontation with Lieutenant Zenkichi now ensued as we tried to negotiate terms with

*Emperor Hirohito recording his surrender speech\*, Tokyo.*

him. As our fate hung in the balance, it was only by Jerry Bunch making direct and timely radio contact with American forces in Tokyo that proved to Zenkichi that any harmful action carried out against the prisoners would be on his head, and his head alone. He, perhaps relieved, saw a way out, backed down and acceded to our terms. All guards were dismissed and we POWs took over administration of the camp to await our final rescue.

One morning, five or six days later, Lieutenant Newton, flying an American reconnaissance fighter plane based on the aircraft carrier *USS Hancock*, spotted our camp. On a second pass, he flew in over us low and slow and dropped instructions for preparing the camp to receive supplies from the air. That afternoon, a squadron of American torpedo planes dropped the first of many parachute-loads of food, medicines, clothes and other supplies that we were to receive over the next month, while waiting for ground troops to arrive.

On September 15, 1945, a month to the day since Emperor Hirohito's surrender, a task force of marines hit at the beach closest to Ohasi and roared up the road and into the camp, armed to the teeth. As we were still in what could be considered "enemy territory," our removal was to be a swift extraction.

The tough-looking marine colonel snapped out orders

*\* Appendix B*

*Ohasi Prisoner of War camp, following liberation, c October 1945.*

to us and to his men for the evacuation to the beach, where reinforcements waited, then said, "Any questions?"

Lieutenant Maxwell Humble, an American prisoner, raised his hand. "Yes sir! What took you so long?" That raised a smile on anxious faces!

After nearly four years in captivity, we were free.

*Epilogue*

Jerry Bunch returned home after the war, married and had a family. He remained in the navy, and rose to become a Lieutenant Commander. He was twice decorated for his bravery during the Korean War. After 23 years of service, he retired in 1958. In 1978 Jerry Bunch was killed in a car crash, of which he was the innocent victim.

I never forgot Jerry Bunch's dedication to his duty to help his prison comrades, his cool effectiveness, and his

114

personal courage. After his tragic death, I and his family felt his valuable, selfless bravery at Ohasi should be recognized posthumously by the United States Navy. To apply for the coveted Navy Cross on Jerry's behalf, his wartime behaviour would have to have been witnessed by, and now testified to, by a superior officer. As his Canadian comrade-in-arms at Ohasi, I was able to proudly fulfill that requirement. My Affidavit follows:

*Jerry Bunch as a post-war Lieutenant Commander United States Navy, c 1957.*

| | | |
|---|---|---|
| **PROVINCE OF ONTARIO** | ) | **IN THE MATTER OF** |
| | ) | |
| | ) | Jerry J. Bunch, Radioman 1st Class, |
| | ) | U.S. Navy |
| | ) | |
| | ) | |

## AFFIDAVIT

I, George MacDonell, of the City of Toronto, in the Province of Ontario, make oath and say as follows:

That during the last war I served in the Canadian Army from September 1939 to March of 1946 in a Canadian Infantry regiment.

I was later discharged from the Army with the rank of Lieutenant.

Following the battle of Hong Kong in December 1941 I became a prisoner of war of the Japanese.

In April of 1945 I was sent with a contingent of my men to the Ohasi prison camp in Northern Japan.

It was here I met a very brave man named Jerry J. Bunch, Radioman 1st class, U.S. Navy, who had served in the U.S. Houston before she was sunk in March 1942 in the Sunda Strait.

Jerry Bunch was an invaluable asset in the Ohasi Camp because he had built, maintained and he operated a clandestine radio which provided us with the news of the outside world. He operated the radio secretly in utter defiance of our captors knowing full well, if discovered, he faced certain torture and execution.

These courageous and voluntary actions were very dangerous and far beyond the call of duty.

Bunch's actions were extremely beneficial to his officers and his fellow prisoners at the isolated Ohasi Camp for the following reasons:

It allowed me and the Senior American officer in the camp to have up-to-date intelligence about the state of the war, and the proximity of allied forces which was an essential basis for an attempted mass escape at the appropriate moment in the impending invasion of Japan. This intelligence was vital to any successful action on our part.

Jerry's radio reception when carefully disseminated was a tremendous boost to morale as he reported via the radio the news of Americans step by step victories in the Pacific on the way to Japan.

I cannot emphasize enough how important Jerry's efforts were in letting us know we were not going to be left to die in Ohasi. He informed us from his radio news that we had a chance of rescue and survival. His courage and skill gave my men the hope so essential to keep going and saved many lives.

When the Emperor gave his surrender speech to the Japanese people on the 15th of August we were then left in a dangerous power vacuum with a Camp Commander who had written orders to kill us if he believed we might be rescued by invading allied forces. When the Japanese Camp Commander learned and we showed him, we were in direct radio contact with U.S. forces in Tokyo through Bunch's radio he dropped his threatening attitude and began to cooperate with us to ensure our safety until the U.S. Marines arrived on the 15th of September. Bunch's radio to an unarmed prison population was a key part of our negotiating power, our safety, and our eventual safe release.

In conclusion as one of Bunch's superiors I cannot say enough in praise of his courage and his patriotism in this dangerous situation.
After all these years I have never heard or known of any braver action by any of those captured by the Japanese than those of Jerry J. Bunch, Radioman, 1st Class of the U. S. Navy. We will never forget him.

I am attaching as an Exhibit "A" to this affidavit a copy of my letter dated November 20, 2006 to Ms. Judy Bunch about the heroics of Jerry Bunch.

SWORN before me at the City of Toronto        )
in the Province of Ontario                              )
this 12th  day of October, 2011                       )
                                                                      )
                                                                      )          George MacDonell
                                                                      )
A Commissioner, etc.                                   )

**Ville K. Masalin**
Barrister & Solicitor
191 Eglinton Avenue East
Suite 309
Toronto, Ontario
Canada  M4P 1K1

# Epilogue

The Japanese military, in their victorious sweep through South East Asia in 1941-42, captured 146,000 Caucasian Prisoners Of War from Great Britain, America, Holland, France, New Zealand, Australia, and Canada.

According to historian Richard B. Franks in his book *Downfall*, the Japanese policy of starvation and abuse led to the death of 46,600 or 33% of those in their prison camps.

The Japanese featured a policy not only to starve their prisoners but also to try to humiliate and dehumanize them until they lost their self-respect and their will to live.

To show defiance towards such an enemy under these conditions requires a person of rare self-confidence, a firm belief in his cause, and unusual courage.

I believe these heretofore untold stories are part of our history – a history we can be proud of.

# Bibliography

Banfill, Dr. Stanley, Diary, Unpublished

Banham, Tony, *Not the Slightest Chance, The Defence of Hong Kong* 1941, U.B.C. Press Vancouver - Toronto.

Dower, John W, Embracing Defeat: Japan in the Wake of World War II (New York: W Morton and Company 1999)

Garneau, Grant: *The Royal Rifles in Hong Kong*: Sherbrooke Quebec: Progressive Publications (1970) Incorporated

Gruhl, Werner, *Imperial Japan's World War Two 1931-1945*: New Brunswick USA: Transaction Publishers

Ross, Lance: Diary: Unpublished

Stacy, C.P.: *Official History of the Canadian Army in the Second World War: Vol 1; Six Years of War: The Army in Canada, Britain and the Pacific* (Queen's Printer Ottawa ON 1960)

Vincent, Carl, *No Reason Why: The Canadian Hong Kong Tragedy*. (Stittsville Ont: Canada Wings Inc 1981)

# Role of Honour

Who lost their lives at Stanley Village
25 December 1941

Adams, Bryce
Baker, John Vincent
Bertrin, Edmonton
Bormier, Frank
Fallow, William
Forsyth, Delmot Wilbam
Hendelson, Elzie
Hanchuk, Harold
Irvine, Bertram
Irvine, Crandel
Kinnie, Ronald
Lafferty, Harvey Reginald
Lyons, Jack
MacLean, Charles
Major, Wilson
Mann, James Burnett
MacClellan, Wendell
McGuire, Ralph
MacKay, John
Mait, Andrew
Mellis, Leo
Noseworthy, Percy
Poag, Russel
Pollack, Frederick
Sheldon, Bertram
Surette, Henry Andrew

# Photo Credits

All other photos from Public Domain.

# Appendix A

Churchill's Message to the Troops in Hong Kong:
December 21, 1941.

*"There must be no thought of surrender. Every part of the island must be fought for and the enemy resisted with the greatest stubbornness. The enemy should be compelled to expend the utmost life and equipment. There must be vigorous fighting in the inner defenses and, if need be, from house to house. Every day you maintain your resistance you help the allied cause all over the world, and by prolonged resistance, you and your men can win the lasting honour which we are sure will be your due."*

# Appendix B

Emperor Hirohito's surrender speech to
the Japanese people on 15 August 1945.

*"After pondering deeply the general trends of the world and the actual
conditions obtaining in our Empire today, we have decided to effect a
settlement of the present situation by resorting to an extraordinary
measure.*

*We have ordered our Government to communicate to the Governments
of the United States, Great Britain, China, and the Soviet Union that
our Empire accepts the provisions of their joint declaration.*

*To strive for the common prosperity and happiness of all nations as well
as the security and well- being of our subjects is the solemn obligation
that has been handed down by our Imperial Ancestors, and we lay it
close to the heart.*

*Indeed, we declared war on America and Britain out of our sincere
desire to ensure Japan's self-preservation and the stabilization of East
Asia, it being far from our thought either to infringe upon the sovereignty
of other nations or to embark upon territorial aggrandizement.*

*But now the war has lasted for nearly four years. Despite the best that
has been done by everyone-- the gallant fighting of the military and naval
forces, the diligence and assiduity of our servants of the state and the
devoted service of our 100 million people--the war situation has
developed not necessarily to Japan's advantage, while the general trends
of the world have all turned against her interest.*

*Moreover, the enemy has begun to employ a new and most cruel bomb,
the power of which to do damage is, indeed, incalculable, taking the toll
of many innocent lives. Should we continue to fight, it would not only
result in an ultimate collapse and obliteration of the Japanese nation,
but also it would lead to the total extinction of human civilization.*

*Such being the case, how are we to save the millions of our subjects, or
to atone ourselves before the hallowed spirits of our Imperial Ancestors?
This is the reason why we have ordered the acceptance of the provisions
of the joint declaration of the powers.*

We cannot but express the deepest sense of regret to our allied nations of East Asia, who have consistently cooperated with the Empire toward the emancipation of East Asia.

The thought of those officers and men as well as others who have fallen in the fields of battle, those who died at their posts of duty, and those who met with death and all their bereaved families, pains our heart night and day.

The welfare of the wounded and the war sufferers, and of those who have lost their homes and livelihood is the object of our profound solicitude. The hardships and suffering to which our nation is to be subjected hereafter will be certainly great.

We are keenly aware of the inmost feelings of all you, our subjects. However, it is according to the dictates of time and fate that we have resolved to pave the way for a grand peace for all the generations to come by enduring the unendurable and suffering what is insufferable. Having been able to save and maintain the structure of the Imperial State, we are always with you, our good and loyal subjects, relying upon your sincerity and integrity.

Beware most strictly of any outbursts of emotion that may engender needless complications, and of any fraternal contention and strife that may create confusion, lead you astray and cause you to lose the confidence of the world.

Let the entire nation continue as one family from generation to generation, ever firm in its faith in the imperishableness of its divine land, and mindful of its heavy burden of responsibilities, and the long road before it. Unite your total strength to be devoted to the construction for the future. Cultivate the ways of rectitude, nobility of spirit, and work with resolution so that you may enhance the innate glory of the Imperial State and keep pace with the progress of the world.

All you, our subjects, we command you to act in accordance with our wishes."

*George MacDonell, The Last Goodbye, Hong Kong 2005.*

*They shall grow not old,*
*as we that are left grow old.*
*Age shall not weary them,*
*nor the years condem.*
*At the going down of the sun,*
*and in the morning*
*We will remember them.*

LAURENCE BINYON

CPSIA information can be obtained
at www.ICGtesting.com
Printed in the USA
FSHW021306311219
65626FS